Engage
How to Know God

Justin R. Jones

ISBN: 1542920086
ISBN-13: 978-1542920087

To my wife Janelle:
Who has demonstrated faithfulness and love far beyond what I deserve. I am thankful to the Lord for you!

To my family:
Who steadfastly modeled how to know God from my childhood to the present. Without their guidance, I am not sure where I would be.

To my Spiritual Formation team:
Who have supported me and stood by my side in this journey. This book wouldn't be here without you!

ACKNOWLEDGMENTS

A big thank you to:

- All those who painstakingly edited the book including: Janelle Jones, C. Ray Miller, and Dawn Waggoner.
- Joni Canastraro for utilizing her amazing design skills to design the cover and the symbols.
- Shawn King and Katie Bartolone for helping me in countless ways to get to the finish line.
- The leaders and staff at Eastern Hills Wesleyan Church for allowing me to pursue this project and supporting me along the way.

CONTENTS

	Acknowledgments	i
1	Introduction	1
2	Step 1: Humbled by God's Eternal Truth	7
3	Step 2: Broken to Have a New Heart	25
4	Step 3: Surrendered to God's Grace	49
5	Step 4: Revived for Authentic Living	71
6	Step 5: Thankful for Growing Relationships	91
7	Step 6: Waiting for Everyone to Be Equipped	121
8	Conclusion: How to Share the Gospel	145
	Notes	152

INTRODUCTION

I was sitting with my wife, Janelle, in a doctor's appointment downtown not long ago. The building was really old and had a small, creaky elevator that slowly took us to a drab third floor waiting room. After sitting there for a while, we were sent down the hallway to an even smaller and more lackluster waiting room. It was one of those waiting rooms that suck the souls out of people with its fluorescent lights, old flowery chairs, and dingy walls. Unsure of how long the appointment would take, I opened my laptop intending to work on some things when something caught my eye. To my surprise I looked up at the ceiling and saw a large, strange-looking moth. How this moth got up an elevator the whole way to the third floor of this fortress-like doctor's office was beyond me. Maybe he came in a window? Whatever the case, this mysterious moth was hanging on to one of the fluorescent lights. I watched him for a while to make sure he didn't swoop down near me and then I returned to my work.

A little while later while I was still waiting for Janelle, I heard a fluttering and looked up to see the moth flying across the room toward the light not far above my head. For a second, everyone paused from whatever they were doing to watch. He buzzed and flitted around the light and continually hit himself against it. I can only assume he was trying to get back outside to the place he was supposed to be, where the gentle breeze would help him fly easily around open fields and the bright sun would bring him warmth. Instead, he was stuck in this terribly depressing place with a light that deceived him into thinking he was outside, causing him to continually hit himself against it until he couldn't anymore. Then he would sit there and regain his strength and try all over again. I was a little sad to think that unless someone intervened, the end of this moth would be in this awful room, continually trying to get out until he didn't have any strength left.

It may seem like a ridiculous waste of time to be watching a moth in a waiting room (although it is a waiting room so anything can become entertainment), but the thought actually popped into my head: this is exactly how many of our lives are. Think about it. God created us with beautiful purpose and design. We are like a beautiful moth and we are meant for "gentle breezes" and "open fields" and the "bright sun." But sin destroyed this purpose for us and in us. And we are left like the moth, trying over and over again to find the things that we really desire: meaning, purpose, and love.

When you don't ultimately find what you're looking for you can feel helpless and want to give up. Some regain their strength after a time (like the moth did) and resume trying to find the things they have always wanted, but no matter how many times they try it doesn't get them anywhere. Others just give up completely and stop trying to find meaning, purpose, and love in this world at all. These people tend to simply live out their life doing what feels right in the moment, often regretting in the long run what they have chosen to do and what their lives have become.

So where can we find hope? Where do we go for answers? What can we do to solve our problem? The only answer to this question is God. Now before you get frustrated, I know you have probably seen many bad examples of what God looks like in the world. Maybe you grew up going to church and the pastor preached a lot of fancy things, but never really lived them out. Maybe you had a family member or friend that claimed they were a believer but they were kind of crazy. Maybe you have seen stories in the news about Christians and you've bought into the hype that they are just self-centered and hypocritical. Maybe your professors told you that only an idiot would think that God existed. Whatever the case, I beg you to put aside that experience no matter how difficult, and engage in the process of finding out what it truly means to know God.

Why? Well, for one, when have you ever trusted that everyone who claims to be someone really is that person? Recently, I saw a commercial where a lady was under the impression that everything she heard on the internet was completely true, and the whole commercial was playing off the many ways that people on the internet can stretch the truth or outright lie. You see, we live in a world of skepticism and it is usually second nature for us to question whether someone is really who they say they are. Yet, ironically, when we meet Christians in our lives we never question whether they are really a follower of Christ. Instead we question the God they claim to follow. I can tell you as a pastor with many years of experience, however, that there are many people who claim to follow God and attend church week after week but their lives demonstrate that they do not know Him personally. So don't believe that because one person or one group of people is a bad representation of God, that God Himself does not exist.

The second reason you should consider engaging in the process of knowing God is that the question of God's existence is the most important question that could be asked of you. Do you really want that question to be answered for you by someone else? What I mean is this: whether or not there is a God has significant consequences for your daily life. If there is no God, then there is no hope beyond this world. We must believe then that we have evolved over the years and are just the products of an undirected and hard world. This also means that there is no absolute moral truth to follow, there is no ultimate meaning and purpose to life, and we should "eat, drink, and be merry for tomorrow we die" like the depressed moth.

But if there is a God, then it means that we are created beings. It means that we were designed for a purpose, that there is an ultimate destiny for our souls after this life, and that there are absolute moral truths that we are to live by. If this is the case, then we better try to get to know who God is so that we can honor Him and live our lives according to what He would desire.

These are two very different views of the world and our lives. Now, why would you want to completely trust the experience and knowledge of one person or a handful of people instead of engaging the question of God on your own and determine for yourself whether He is real or not? We do this all the time in far less important things. Recently, a new superhero movie came out and I wondered how it was. I checked social media, I talked to my friends who would have seen it, and I read some reviews. You know what I found? Everyone had a different opinion. If I wanted to really find out how it was, then I needed to go experience the movie myself. If we do that for such small things, why would we not want to experience God ourselves and make a decision based on that?

So I invite you to *engage* in the process of how to know God. I use that word "engage" intentionally because it is a word that is full of meaning for the church where I pastor. Our mission statement is "to engage every person to become a passionate follower of Jesus Christ." We have also used the acronym ENGAGE to define our core values: Eternal Truth, New Heart, God's Grace, Authentic Living, Growing Relationships, and Everybody Equipped. We intentionally use this word repeatedly because we believe in transformation of the heart and life. We believe God wants to transform our lives and the lives of people around us into something beautiful. But we understand that nothing happens by accident. To change we need to intentionally direct our actions and attention in a particular way. For example, if the captain of a ship decides he wants to change course he doesn't just think about it or talk about it. He engages his attention on the map and then takes action to make it happen. In the same way, we believe that to know God we have to actively seek him and receive what he has for us. We believe in the beautiful promise that God says in Jeremiah 29:13, "You will seek me and find me when you seek me with all your heart." This book endeavors to show you the steps to engage with God and what it means to know Him, and I pray that you take this opportunity to truly do that.

The book is broken into six separate steps that the Bible says are part of coming to know God. I have used the word ENGAGE as an acronym for this process and have attached an action verb that demonstrates how we are called to engage in each step. Here are the steps that we will consider in this book:

- Humbled by God's ETERNAL TRUTH
- Broken to have a NEW HEART
- Surrendered to GOD'S GRACE
- Revived for AUTHENTIC LIVING
- Thankful for GROWING RELATIONSHIPS
- Waiting for EVERYONE to be EQUIPPED

The goal is for you to study each of these steps and to engage in the heart steps that are listed at the end of each chapter. I have found the best way to pursue these steps is to do them in the context of community. So if you are not reading this with someone else, then choose someone and invite him or her into the journey. At the end of every chapter there will be questions to help start conversations. I pray that God will give you insight as you seek Him!

Step 1
HUMBLED BY GOD'S ETERNAL TRUTH

Have you ever really stopped to gaze at the stars at night? Have you ever sat and watched the sunrise or sunset? Have you ever studied the plants and flowers around you and the bugs that crawl along the ground? What is the feeling you get when you've done these things?

I sat in the midst of a Ugandan town on a mission trip when I was in college and was overwhelmed by the stars. Some friends and I were there to minister to some of the kids in an area that had at one time been disrupted by the Lord's Resistance Army. We were staying with local missionaries and one thing I figured out quickly is that electricity was a very fickle thing in that region. It was more common for the power to be out than for it to be on. There were some definite downsides to not having electricity, but one of the more amazing experiences of my life happened as a result of there being no power. One night our whole team grabbed chairs and went outside to watch the stars. We were already in a place with very little light pollution and then with the electricity out, there was no light pollution at all. I had never seen anything like it. You could see the shape of the entire galaxy. There were countless stars, with constellations as clear as I'd ever seen them. And I am convinced that we even saw the International Space Station as it moved through the night sky.

What was my reaction to this amazing sight? Wonder, awe, and feeling ultimately humbled. You see, it is in those breathtaking moments that things become crystal clear and you are brought back to reality. All too often my life gets absorbed with to-do lists and the so-called "important things of life" and my world becomes so small. If I am not careful I can start to take myself too seriously, like my life is really "that important," my thoughts are really "that amazing," and "I've got this whole 'life thing' down pretty well." But then reality hits me in the moments I am looking at the stars or the sunrise or God's creation around me. I am so extremely small and insignificant in the grand scheme of things!

Consider some of these statistics. Scientists believe the observable universe to be around 93 billion light-years big, although it continues to expand. A light-year is close to six trillion miles – 6,000,000,000 miles.[1] We live in the Milky Way Galaxy, but there are estimated to be 500 billion other galaxies in the universe. This means that they estimate there to be 50,000,000,000,000,000,000,000 (5×10^{22}) habitable planets in the universe.[2] For our modern spacecraft to reach the nearest star from us, it would take approximately 78,000 years.[3] And scientists estimate we can only see 4% of what makes up the universe. The other 96% is made up of something we cannot see that they call dark energy and dark matter.[4]

Feel small yet? Does it amaze you to think that you are a microscopic piece of this incredibly massive universe? Does it make you question how strongly you depend on your own thoughts and ideas? Does it direct your attention to the great, unknown depths of what you don't know, and leave you open to considering that someone else may hold the truth of what is going on? If so, then you have experienced the very edges of what it means to be humbled. You see, so often we think that humility is thinking less of who we are, but it is something quite different. C.S. Lewis wisely said, "True humility is not thinking less of yourself; it is thinking of yourself less."[5] True humility begins when we stop thinking about ourselves constantly, refrain from believing that our thoughts are special in some way, and intentionally make room for thinking about things that are beyond us.

According to the Bible, humility is an important first step in the process of knowing God. Considers these scriptures:

"...if my people, who are called by my name, will **humble** themselves and pray and seek my face and turn from their wicked ways, then I will hear from heaven, and I will forgive their sin and will heal their land."–2 Chronicles 7:14

"Because your heart was responsive and you **humbled** yourself before God when you heard what he spoke against this place and its people, and because you **humbled** yourself before me and tore your robes and wept in my presence, I have heard you, declares the LORD." – 2 Chronicles 34:27

"You save the **humble** but bring low those whose eyes are haughty." – Psalm 18:27

"He guides the **humble** in what is right and teaches them his way." – Psalm 25:9

"For those who exalt themselves will be **humbled**, and those who **humble** themselves will be exalted." – Matthew 23:12

"Be completely **humble** and gentle; be patient, bearing with one another in love." – Ephesians 4:2

"And being found in appearance as a man, he **humbled** himself by becoming obedient to death— even death on a cross!" – Philippians 2:8

"**Humble** yourselves, therefore, under God's mighty hand, that he may lift you up in due time." – 1 Peter 5:6

Obviously there seems to be a connection in the Bible between humility and our ability to relate to God, but what are we to be humbled by in particular? In order to know God we must be humbled enough to admit three things:

- There is absolute moral TRUTH that isn't based solely on what I think or feel.
- There is an ETERNITY beyond this world with which I have to come to terms.
- There is a God who created me and has the ANSWERS I've been looking for.

TRUTH

First, let's start with this claim: "There is absolute moral truth that isn't based solely on what I think or feel." For much of history this would have been an absurd statement because most people would have believed in an absolute truth beyond themselves. They would have believed in an absolute right and wrong that undergirded all moral and ethical decisions.

In today's relativistic culture, however, this belief in an absolute truth has been replaced with individualistic truth. After the philosophers of the nineteenth and twentieth century declared "God is dead" it was only a matter of time for absolute truth to be replaced with a "truth" that is defined by what I want it to be. Today, it is common to hear someone say, "Believe what feels right to you and I'll believe what feels right to me." Perhaps you may believe this to some extent, but there are many problems with living out this kind of perspective.

First, if we look at it purely from a logical standpoint, it puts us on shaky ground. Ponder this: The letter "A" does not make a particular sound because I feel like it should. It makes that sound because that is how the letter "A" is defined. Take math as another example: $2 + 2 = 4$ and that is not because I feel it should. It equals 4 because that is how the numbers are defined and how addition works. Grass is green whether I want it to be or not, and water is produced by two hydrogen atoms and one oxygen atom whether I want it to be or not. There are defined and discernable truths that are true no matter what we feel.

Still, when many of us look at the world in a moral and spiritual framework, we decide we should throw out this idea that certain things are true and certain things are false. We determine that everyone should personally conclude what sin is and is not, what love is and is not, and what the true meaning of life is and is not. It is treated completely differently from any other search for truth. Instead of pursuing the person and resources that could provide us with an answer about what sin is and what love is, we decide it on our own by our personal feelings and thoughts. We make up our mind that we and no one else will define our moral and spiritual lives.

However, if we really stop to think about this, it should scare us. We should be afraid about how prideful we are in assuming that our intuition and thoughts are that accurate. Honestly consider what we talked about in the beginning of the chapter. We are microscopic in terms of the universe. And think about how little knowledge we actually possess. Take all the things about the universe that have ever been known. What percentage do you think you know? Maybe 1-2% at the most. Maybe you have a doctorate or are a rocket scientist and that number could jump to 3-4%. Are you willing to bet with that little amount of information, you just naturally have the answers to the meaning of life and what is right and wrong?

Can you imagine taking a similar stance in any other area of life? Imagine you just found out that you require surgery. Are you going to tell the doctor to get the surgical room ready because you will perform the surgery yourself? Would you get on an airplane and tell the pilot that he can take a break because you are ready to take over the rest of the flight? We need to come to terms with the fact that we should have humility in determining whether we really know what is right and wrong. And we need to consider there is absolute moral truth that is true whether we want it to be or not.

This is essential if we are to know God. In 1 Corinthians 1:25 the Bible says, "For the foolishness of God is wiser than man's wisdom, and the weakness of God is stronger than man's strength." In Isaiah 55:8-9 it says, "'For my thoughts are not your thoughts, neither are your ways my ways,' declares the Lord. 'As the heavens are higher than the earth, so are my ways higher than your ways and my thoughts than your thoughts.'" If there really is a God out there then to be God He must be far more amazing than we are. We can imagine that even His "foolishness" would be wiser than our greatest thoughts and His ways would be greater than even our greatest acts. If that is the case and we are truly seeking to know God, then we must start by being humbled to believe "there is absolute moral truth that isn't based solely on what I think or feel."

ETERNITY

The second statement we need to be humbled enough to admit is: "There is an ETERNITY beyond this world with which I have to come to terms." Earlier in this chapter I stated many statistics that demonstrate the magnitude of the universe. It is incredible to think about how vast this physical universe really is, but suppose that what we can physically see is not all there is? What if there is a greater reality beyond this physical universe?

Many scientists and scholars will tell you this is ridiculous. There is nothing beyond what is observable they would remark, but let's do a little thought experiment to see if this is true. Most scientists or scholars would tell you that there was a point in history called the Big Bang. According to them this was a moment when the entire universe exploded into existence from a single point and started to expand. Many of these same scientists would declare that creation of the universe by God is a hoax. However, what they are saying happened scientifically is almost identical to what we say happened when God created the universe – that something (the universe) came from nothing. The problem scientists have is that they wouldn't be able to tell you the reason why something came from nothing and those of us who believe the Bible's story of creation can.

You see, we can all understand that something doesn't come from nothing without something or someone causing it. Growing up, if I smelled something amazing and came into the kitchen to see a steaming hot apple pie on top of the oven, I wouldn't say, "This pie spontaneously appeared out of nowhere " or "I wonder where this pie came from?" I would assume that my mom had baked the pie and it was sitting there cooling.

Now, consider the universe. Either the universe is eternal, meaning it has always existed and will forever exist, and in that case there is no need for someone to have started it. Or the universe is finite, meaning it had a starting point and will have an ending point, and in that case there needs to be something or someone outside of the universe that is eternal and started it. This just makes sense, doesn't it? Something does not come from nothing unless someone or something causes it.

So if scientists and scholars say there seems to have been a start to the universe based on scientific knowledge and there seems to be a time in history when the universe will end, how can we not assume there is something outside of the universe that is eternal? In our case, we believe God is the Eternal One and that we have to come to terms with this eternal God if we are to know whether or not we will dwell with Him after our time on earth is done.

These conclusions have been based on thinking through the question, but the Bible confirms what we have discussed about eternity. In Revelation 1:8 it says, "'I am the Alpha and the Omega,' says the Lord God, 'who is, and who was, and who is to come, the Almighty.'" God declares Himself to be the Eternal One who always has existed and who always will exist. In another passage, Ecclesiastes 3:11, it says, "He has made everything beautiful in its time. He has also set eternity in the hearts of men; yet they cannot fathom what God has done from beginning to end." In this God is saying that deep down we know there is something more to our existence than just the world we see.

Maybe you have already felt this tug on your heart before. Maybe you have been living most of your life without much thought to what is really going on around you. I have talked to many people over the years who say they have never really thought about ideas like eternity or what happens to them after they die, but at the same time when we start to talk about it you can tell it connects with something deep within them. Even though they have never intentionally thought about it, there is a yearning inside of them to have their existence be something more than just the daily drama and problems of this life.

Until we are willing to acknowledge "there is an ETERNITY beyond this world with which we have to come to terms," we can never start the process of knowing God. Because if we want to know God then it is imperative to understand that we are talking about knowing an eternal being. We have to be willing to ask ourselves what our eternal destiny really is, and whether knowing God is our way of being confident of our eternal destiny.

ANSWERS

Finally, if we are really going to know God, we must be humbled enough to believe that "There is a God who created me and has the ANSWERS I've been looking for." We have skirted around the issue this entire chapter, but up until this point I haven't asked you to truly answer the question whether you believe there is a God that created you. You could believe in absolute truth and eternity and yet have some other theory about how all of these things came to be. However, believing in a creator God who has the answers we are looking for is the most probable answer and we simply have to be willing to be humbled enough to accept it. Romans 1:20-25 describes the situation well. It says:

For since the creation of the world God's invisible qualities – his eternal power and divine nature – have been clearly seen, being understood from what has been made, so that men are without excuse. For although they knew God, they neither glorified him as God nor gave thanks to him, but their thinking became futile and their foolish hearts were darkened. Although they claimed to be wise, they became fools and exchanged the glory of the immortal God for images made to look like mortal man and birds and animals and reptiles. Therefore God gave them over in the sinful desires of their hearts to sexual impurity for the degrading of their bodies with one another. They exchanged the truth of God for a lie, and worshipped and served created things rather than the Creator – who is forever praised. Amen.

This passage affirms that when we consider there are absolute moral truths that need to be understood and when we consider the great vastness of the universe that was created by someone, we have to assume that this was God's doing. And this passage points out that we know it in our hearts as well. Deep down we know that there is someone out there that has created all of this and who has answers to our questions.

The problem, which we will discuss in depth in the next chapter, is that we don't want to admit it. In our pride, we hold onto our own perception of reality and would rather do what we want with our lives instead of seeking out what God, who created us, wants us to do. As the passage says, "Although they claimed to be wise, they became fools and exchanged the glory of the immortal God for images made to look like mortal man and birds and animals and reptiles" (Romans 1:22-23). At the time Romans was written, people would actually worship idols made of wood or stone that looked like animals or men or god-like figures. You might hear that and laugh and wonder how that applies to today. But really are the idols of today any different? An idol can be anything that we spend all of our energy, time, and money on instead of seeking God. Maybe you don't worship an animal statue, but you might be worshipping one or more of these things: money, sex, family, work, a hobby, an actor or actress, material possessions, alcohol, food, yourself…the list goes on.

When we choose to depend on our own feelings or desires, we end up as the passage says, "They exchanged the truth of God for a lie, and worshipped and served created things rather than the Creator – who is forever praised. Amen." The problem is that for those of us who have come to this realization, we realize these idols do not really satisfy us. Maybe we devote our entire lives to our careers and we work tirelessly to the point of even neglecting our families and other important things. What does it get us? A momentary sense of satisfaction, material possessions, or a feeling of purpose? It may feel good for a moment, but if our work is what we are worshipping what happens when that job is gone? What does all that time and energy mean for eternity if we were simply working for ourselves?

Or consider something like sex or alcohol or a devotion to food or money. Maybe doing whatever it takes to get those things feels good for a moment, but does it really satisfy you in the long haul? Ask yourself for a moment if filling your time with these things will answer the deep questions of life, meaning, and purpose? Will you truly be satisfied if these things define your life?

If we're honest, I think the answer for all of us is "no." If you are willing to come to this conclusion as well, then you must be humbled to believe that "There is a God who created me and has the ANSWERS I've been looking for." And if you are willing to acknowledge this statement you can truly start the journey of knowing God. You are finally willing to listen instead of speak. You are finally willing to be humbled and acknowledge that you are not the center of the universe. You are finally willing to seek what God might want for you instead of assume. It might seem like a negative thing to you at first, but it is truly a place of great freedom. No longer do you have to answer all the world's problems and issues. You can acknowledge that you don't have all the answers and turn to the God Who does.

How Do I Become Humbled by God's Eternal Truth?

Acknowledging that we have to be humbled does not mean that we know how to be humbled. We are often humbled by circumstances instead of choosing to humble ourselves. When I was in middle school, I was a pianist for our school chorus.

Some of the school district music teachers would make comments about me being a skilled pianist because I was playing songs beyond my grade level. I started to get prideful about this, especially when I was given a piece that was harder than anyone my age had played for our next school concert. I worked and worked on that piece and I think it was partially because I wanted people to see how talented I was and praise me for it. I was in the middle of playing the song at the concert and a page turn went wrong. I didn't have the piece memorized and I was so confused where I was that I missed playing at least a third of the song. Needless to say I was humbled through this experience, but it was not something I would have chosen.

Choosing to be humbled is a completely different thing entirely. There are at least three different practical ways that we can humble ourselves before God:

1. PRAYER: Acknowledge through prayer that you don't have all the answers.

Now, this might sound strange to you if you have never prayed before, but the first thing to do if you believe there might be a God is to tell Him that you are willing to stop depending on your own answers and are willing to hear from Him. In James 4 where it talks about being humbled before God, it says, "Come near to God and he will come near to you" (James 4:8). If you are willing to tell Him that you are searching for Him and that you simply want the honest truth about Who He is and what life is about, He promises to come near to you.

If you have never prayed or have not prayed often throughout your life, then it is as simple as talking to God honestly. It might feel weird that you are talking to someone you can't see, but simply go somewhere comfortable, close your eyes, and talk to God as though He is sitting there with you because He is. Then listen for His voice. Again, it might feel weird, but what's the worst that could happen? I have heard so many testimonies of people that were willing to be humbled and God started showing up in their life.

2. THE BIBLE: Acknowledge that you're willing to search for answers by starting to read the Bible.

Maybe you have never read the Bible before or you've simply read bits and pieces. One of the easiest ways to humble yourself and be willing to know God is to start reading the Bible and see what it really says. I would suggest starting to read the Gospels in the New Testament if you've never read the Bible. Many suggest that the Gospel of John is one of the easiest books to start reading. Now, I am not asking you to simply be indoctrinated by reading it and believing it without any questions. I would encourage you to keep a note pad next to you as you read and write down any questions or thoughts you have. One of my favorite authors, G.K. Chesterton, wrote, "The Christian Ideal has not been tried and found wanting; it has been found difficult and left untried."[6] I am convinced that most people know a lot about what other people have said about the Bible, but they don't really know what is actually in the Bible. Most have never read it and tested it for themselves (as Chesterton alludes to). I encourage you to truly test the Bible. You have already told God through prayer that you are willing to accept His Truth if He is real, so seek God through the Bible and see if it makes sense.

I encourage you to find someone, whether it is a Christian

friend or pastor, who knows God and who is knowledgeable about the Bible and ask him or her if you can sit with them over coffee or a meal and ask them all your questions. They might not have all the answers, but it would be a good start. Also, if you find a local Bible-believing church that has classes on studying the Bible, I encourage you to attend those classes and start learning what the Bible really says.

3. QUESTIONS: Acknowledge through questions that you might not have all the answers.

It seems like a simple thing, but many of us do not ask many questions of our lives. We simply live. A good way to be humbled is to start asking yourself whether what you are doing is right and apply what you are learning through prayer and the Bible to these situations. For instance, if you are known as the gossip at work, instead of excusing away why you gossip, start to ask yourself if gossiping is the right thing to do and why you do it in the first place. Or if you have an idol in your life (something that consumes most of your time, money, and energy) ask yourself whether it is right to focus your entire life around this thing and why you do that in the first place? The act of questioning your own assumptions and actions demonstrates that you are willing to be humbled by God. At the beginning of James 4 it says:

What causes fights and quarrels among you? Don't they come from your desires that battle within you? You want something but don't get it. You kill and covet, but you cannot have what you want. You quarrel and fight. You do not have, because you do not ask God. When you ask, you do not receive, because you ask with wrong motives, that you may spend what you get on your pleasures.

It is important that we ask questions of our actions and our motives, and then ask God about them. We do this by asking God through prayer to show us what is right and to seek answers in the Bible about what God thinks about those things.

If you are willing to intentionally be humbled by God's Eternal Truth then you are on your way to knowing God, but this is only the first step. It is important to understand, however, that this may possibly be the most important step. Only when we are willing to be humbled do we have any hope of knowing who God truly is. You might even be reading this book and think that you already know who God is so this doesn't apply to you. But I have known many people who have claimed to know God for years who are completely self-righteous and are not humble in their attitude toward God. They use God to get what they want. Their spiritual life is simply a religion that they use to make themselves feel better while they live however they want with no real humility to listen to God. If this is you, then I would ask you to consider whether you have ever really been humbled by God's Eternal Truth. It is the beginning of knowing God, but also the beginning of true freedom, because as Augustine once said, "...Our hearts are restless till they find rest in Thee (God)."[7]

REFLECTION QUESTIONS

1. When is the last time you experienced wonder and awe? What was it about that experience that produced wonder and awe in you?
2. Do you find it easy to become self-absorbed and not consider the bigger picture? Why?

3. Lewis said, "True humility is not thinking less of yourself; it is thinking of yourself less." Have you ever thought about humility in this way before?

4. TRUTH – One of the things we have to be humbled by is that there is absolute truth not based solely on what we think or feel. This seems to contradict the popular opinions of the day. Why do you think our society has such a hard time accepting this?

5. ETERNITY – Do you believe in eternity? If so, how often do you think about eternity in your everyday life?

6. ANSWERS – Sometimes, even if we believe in truth and eternity, we would still rather go our own way instead of depending on God for answers. Have you ever experienced this in your life and did going your own way really produce purpose, meaning, and joy?

7. Which one of the application steps below will be most difficult for you?

APPLICATION

1. PRAY – Even if you have never prayed before in your life, take some time to talk to God.

2. BIBLE – Read the Bible and test it to see if it is true. If you have never read before, start in the Gospel of John and keep a pen and paper handy for questions you have about it.

3. QUESTIONS – Start to ask yourself questions about what you believe.

ENGAGE

Step 2
BROKEN TO HAVE A NEW HEART

Being humbled by God's Eternal Truth is only the first step to knowing God. The second step is to be broken to have a new heart. According to United Network for Organ Sharing there have been over 65,000 heart transplants since 1988.[8] Think of the immense importance of a heart transplant. The heart is the center of what makes your body run, the vital center of our physical life. Tens of thousands of lives have been saved because doctors discovered how to give people a new heart.

What if I were to tell you that you are in the same position in which these transplant patients find themselves? You are in need of a new heart as well. I'm not talking about a physical heart, but a heart in the way that the Bible conveys. Cowen describes the concept of the heart in the Bible as "the center of the physical, mental, and spiritual life of a person."[9]

The heart is described as the seat of will and deliberation, the center of feeling and emotion, and the center of moral decisions. There is no word for "conscience" in Hebrew, so when the Bible describes the conscience, the word "heart" is used.

We use many different terms to describe all of these aspects of our human nature. We might differentiate between our heart and our mind, and our will and our feelings. But the Bible seems to combine many of these concepts together in the word for "heart." This understanding of heart is really meant to describe who we are at the very core.

But here's the thing: according to the Bible, our heart is dead and we need a "heart transplant." If we want to know God, then we need to come to terms with this reality and be broken to have a new heart. You might argue that you already do pretty well with controlling your will, emotions, and moral decisions. You might say, "I'm a good person so why would I need a new heart?" So in this chapter we are going to look at this claim and figure out why we need to engage in the process of getting a new heart.

WHY DO WE NEED A NEW HEART?

At the center of this discussion about needing a new heart, we must start by defining what sin is and where it started. Sin is described in the Bible several different ways, but one of the common words used to describe it translates as "missing the mark." So in a very simplified sense, sin is missing out on the way that God desires us to live. If we use an example of a bow and arrow to explain the concept, it is like continually aiming at the target and missing the bull's eye. Sin is making choices and living a life where we are disobeying God's direction and missing out on what He wants for us. Many of you reading this may say, "That doesn't mean much to me because I generally am a pretty good person. The few things God and I might disagree about can't be that big of a deal." But let's go back to the beginning for a deeper look at what sin is and what happened when it came into the world.

According to the Bible, God created everything and it was "good" (Genesis 1:1-25). It was exactly the way He wanted it to be. Then, he created humans, Adam and Eve, and he called them "very good" (Genesis 1:26-31). We were created in God's image, meaning we were created as a reflection of who He is. If I were to put baby pictures of my dad, myself, and my son side by side, it would be difficult to tell them apart. The resemblance is pretty extraordinary. It's similar when you think of our resemblance to God except not necessarily in a physical sense. He created us in His image with a heart like His: with a desire to love, to think, to create, and to care for things.

The Bible says that God placed Adam and Eve in the Garden of Eden to enjoy it and look after it. It was a place of complete peace, freedom, and contentment, a place where they could walk with God and live out their purpose. It was a place free of shame, guilt, and pain. There was only one command that God put in place. God had put two special trees in the garden: the tree of life and the tree of the knowledge of good and evil. In Genesis 2:16-17 it says, "And the LORD God commanded the man, 'You are free to eat from any tree in the garden; but you must not eat from the tree of the knowledge of good and evil, for when you eat from it you will certainly die.'" It was one simple command made for the good of Adam and Eve.

It is in the reaction to this command that sin in our hearts was born. It all started with Satan approaching the woman, Eve, in the form of a snake. He came with a simple question in Genesis 3:1 that doomed Eve and still dooms us all, "Did God really say, 'You must not eat from any tree in the garden?'" Such a simple phrase, "Did God really say," and yet it holds the key to the brokenness of our hearts. You see, in that moment Eve was tempted to doubt God and who He was. Satan was trying to convince her that God did not really love her and that she needed to look out for herself. As she responds in this same section of Scripture you can see her defenses start to go up and the wheels start to turn. She starts to believe the temptation and wonders, "Maybe God doesn't really care for us the way we thought He did."

Genesis 3:6 says, "When the woman saw that the fruit of the tree was good for food and pleasing to the eye, and also desirable for gaining wisdom, she took some and ate it." She reasoned through it and decided it was in her best interest to take some of the fruit from the tree even though God had told them not to eat it. She also gave the fruit to Adam. The effects were immediate. In verse 7 it says, "Then the eyes of both of them were open and they realized they were naked." Before this time, there was simple innocence in the hearts of Adam and Eve. They were completely naked and not ashamed about it. Immediately after doing what God had commanded them not to do, however, shame and guilt flooded into their souls. Not only that, but in fear they ran, tried to hide, and started to blame one another for their problems.

Many years ago, during my college breaks, I worked for a tech company that did video and audio work for giant orthopedic companies. One day I was there by myself working on a big project. I was still learning some of the computer applications used to edit the audio and video clips and I accidentally deleted an entire giant file. The deadline for the project was quickly approaching and I had completely deleted an important part of it. I remember being too terrified to call my boss. Instead, I frantically searched the computer for answers on how to get the file back. I went so far as to purchase some recovery software to get the information back but nothing I was doing seemed to work. Thankfully, another coworker of mine was able to get things back to normal, but I hate remembering the feeling I had when that all happened. I was terrified and ashamed. I wanted to hide in a hole. I didn't want to tell the person to whom I was responsible.

Now, I have experienced that feeling of shame and fear many times before because I am a broken person that lives in a broken world. I have done things I have regretted. But imagine if you were Adam and Eve. They had always lived in perfect peace with God and had never sinned against Him. Now, they had gone against the one command he had given them. Before they sinned they had trusted God, and the weight of the world was on His shoulders and He could handle it. Now, the weight of the world was on their shoulders because they had chosen to stop trusting the One who created them. If you look at Satan's temptation and Eve's response you see the heart of sin and how it caused our broken hearts. The heart of sin is selfishness – to care more about ourselves and what we desire than what God, the One who created us, desires. Satan tried to convince Eve that God couldn't be trusted and Eve thought she could gain something she didn't have. St. Augustine and others would call this the soul being curved inward.

The sad part of making a sinful choice and living a sinful life is that sin is a terrible deception. It always promises satisfaction but leaves you emptier than before. I always seem to experience this deception when I go to Cheesecake Factory. If you have ever been there, you know that the menu is the size of a book and everything you order is huge and delicious. I always enjoy whatever I order, but the place is specifically known for its cheesecake. So since we're not there often, I always think that even though I am full from the meal, I should order a piece of cheesecake to share with my wife. When we get the cheesecake it always tastes amazing, but within a couple minutes I start regretting the choice to order it. I cross that line from full to food-coma to feeling sick. And I tell myself that the next time I come back I won't get cheesecake. But the next time comes around and I do the same thing I did before.

Now, this is just a silly example but sin functions in the same way. In Eve's case, the fruit looked good and seemed like it promised great wisdom and power. Instead, it brought shame, fear, and pain. We can see this same pattern of sin in our own lives. Maybe you choose to gossip, thinking that by gossiping about someone else it will make you feel better about yourself. It never does, however, and instead provides more drama and frustration. Maybe you go to the computer for sexual satisfaction, but it always leaves you wanting more instead of less. You go to drugs and alcohol to forget, but after the hangover you remember everything and feel worse than you did before. You lie, cheat, steal, and get angry because you think it will get you something you don't have. But in the end, it destroys you and others around you. Sin is missing the mark, living with our lives turned in upon ourselves, focused more on what we want instead of what God wants. And if we let sin rule in our lives, it only leads to emptiness.

THE HEART AND SIN

You might say, "Okay, so I probably do sin sometimes and do things that go against what God wants. I might even recognize that those decisions leave me empty inside, but why does that mean that I have to have a completely new heart. I like the way I am." At the core of this statement is a feeling that we can't possibly be that bad. We might look at other people and judge their hearts as being bad. We look at people like serial killers, terrorists, and other bad criminals and say, "Obviously, these people have sinful hearts." We might even look at one of our coworkers, family members, or acquaintances and say, "I can't believe that person. He never thinks of anyone but himself. He is so terrible." But we always give ourselves the benefit of the doubt. You might say, "I may lie sometimes, but I have a reason for doing it. I might cheat sometimes, but everybody else does too. I might gossip about people, but they really are terrible people so they deserve it. I am not really that bad."

The Bible seems to say something different about our situation. Within just a couple chapters of the fall of man in the book of Genesis, it says in Genesis 6:5, "The Lord saw how great man's wickedness on the earth had become, and that every inclination of the thoughts of his heart was only evil all the time." This starts a common theme throughout the Bible, that the first act of sin by Adam and Eve did something more substantial than just cause us to do some bad things here and there. Ultimately, it caused our hearts to be corrupted by sin. Remember how we discussed that the heart was the seat of the will and emotion and moral decision-making? After Adam and Eve chose to disobey God, each one of us was born with corrupted and sinful hearts. This is called "original sin." It became our natural inclination to be sinful instead of following what God would desire for us.

This is obvious to see when you watch a group of young children. Recently, we took our preschool-age son and my sister's three kids to a children's museum, and as you would expect children were everywhere. It was obvious as you watched them with their parents that it is in our nature to sin from the time we are born. The children wanted what they shouldn't have and would fight their parents for it. Some would push other children they didn't like. Others would yell and fight over toys. Even our own family's children had a hard time listening and sharing. Many parents were having that all too familiar altercation where they told their child not to grab something and the child would put their hand on whatever they weren't supposed to grab, and look at their parent with those eyes that are saying, "What are you going to do about it?" It is so obvious that this sinful, rebellious, selfish spirit is in each one of us from the youngest of ages. So sin is not just something we do, it is something that is in our nature when we are born. It is our natural inclination to turn away from the right and healthy things that God would want for us and to turn toward selfishness.

Not only is sin part of our nature, but according to what we read in the Bible and what we see in real life sin leads to death. In Genesis 2:16-17 God warns Adam and Eve that eating the fruit from the tree of the knowledge of good and evil would lead to death. And it did lead to their physical death. Instead of living forever with God, their bodies deteriorated and they died. Death has become the guarantee for each one of us from that time forward because of sin. It says in Romans 5:12, "Therefore, just as sin entered the world through one man (Adam), and death through sin, and in this way death came to all men, because all sinned…" Physical death is one of the guarantees of life that we can't escape.

Sin doesn't just bring about physical death however. The deterioration and death is deeper. Just a generation after Adam and Eve they saw the ramifications of this sinful decay in their souls. Their sons Cain and Abel presented offerings to the Lord. Abel's offering was looked on with favor and Cain's offering was not because he chose to give God a careless offering instead of the best of what He could give like Abel. Cain became angry and jealous that his brother's offering was seen with favor. So God says to him in Genesis 4:6-7, "Why are you angry? Why is your face downcast? If you do what is right, will you not be accepted? But if you do not do what is right, sin is crouching at your door; it desires to have you, but you must rule over it." Sin is personified as sitting at the door of his heart, seeking to destroy him. Instead of listening and turning toward God, the decay of sin brought about death when Cain killed his brother in a field because of his anger.

In our own time and in our own lives, this death and decay of sin is evident all around us. This past year, I saw a news video about drug addicts who were addicted to a drug called "krokodil."[10] It broke my heart because it perfectly demonstrated the death-producing quality of sin. The interview was with a young lady who was a producer of the drug and also a user. She was skin and bones and looked sickly. There was no joy in her face, just a tired restlessness. The photos of other users and the living conditions they were in broke my heart. The addicts talked about how many people they had lost through overdose with what seemed like both deep regret and a sense of their own inevitable destination. Part of the reason it broke my heart so badly was because it perfectly represented what sin does to us. We are like addicts who are addicted to our idols, our control, and our rebellion. The addiction is so intense that we can't even see what life would look like outside of it. We walk around with the death-producing consequences of that sin evident in our lives: broken relationships, restless hearts, and destructive patterns. Sometimes, it shocks me when I talk to people whose relationships and lives are falling apart and they can't seem to see that their own sin has played a part in it. Just like an addict who denies their addiction, so many of these people talk about how they are good people who do some bad things sometimes instead of recognizing the true reality of sin in their lives. They don't feel like they deserve the consequences they are suffering. But if we are ever going to move on toward knowing God and finding freedom, we must be willing to acknowledge our own responsibility in this sinful, chaotic world. We must be willing to acknowledge what it says in Romans 3:23, "all have sinned and fall short of the glory of God," including myself. And this means that we need a new heart.

GOOD WORKS

So at this point, you might be willing to admit that you have a sinful nature and that you need a new heart. But usually our response to discovering that our heart is sinful is to say, "Can't I just make myself have a better heart?" The argument often is: "Well, I can just start living a really, really good life from this point forward, doing all the things that God would want me to do." This is how most people throughout history have tried to deal with sin – do enough good works to make God happy with you and overcome your sin. In fact, it is the underlying assumption of almost any religion you can find. If I do enough good works the higher power I am serving will overlook my bad heart. This never works, however, and we see this demonstrated in how the people of God respond in the Old Testament. They had the Ten Commandments and other guidelines concerning how to follow God and they simply tried to live according to those laws as best they could. However, there are a couple problems with this plan.

First, hopefully in this chapter you've picked up on the reality that sin is pervasive. It infects everything with which it comes in contact. I was on a trip with my wind ensemble during college. We were traveling back to our school after some final concerts and it was going to be a long trip. We were in the middle of the trip when we heard someone throwing up in the back of the bus. It was gross, but it was not completely out of the ordinary to have someone not feeling well during a long trip like that. But then another person started getting sick and then another and by the time we stopped there were people all over the place throwing up. It got so bad that we were passing trash bags up and down the aisles as people got sick. We ended up having to stop at a hotel that night instead of finishing the trip. By the time we had gotten back to the school, almost every single person in our group had gotten sick. Even people that were generally very healthy and were trying to take proper precautions got sick.

Sin functions in a similar way. Even if we try to overcome it with good works, it is so infectious that it even starts to infect the good things we do, making them about ourselves instead of selfless love. This does not mean that someone can never do good works apart from knowing God, but it means that those good works might still miss the mark of what God would want for us. Remember, sin is not just about good deeds versus bad deeds on an imaginary scale. It is about the breakdown of obedience in a relationship. Imagine if when my son gets a little older, I asked him to stay in for the night to study for school. Instead of staying in for the night, he went out with some friends. When he came back that night, he might make the case that while he was out with his friends they decided to help an old lady cross the street and they picked up some garbage along the way. Although I might be happy that my son thought of doing those things, do you think it would matter to me in that moment what he had chosen to do with his friends? I had asked him to stay in for the night and he had disobeyed. So, although we might do some good works sometimes, unless something changes inside of us those good works will still be done in the context of disobedience and rebellion against God.

Second, even if we tried to do good works all of our life, the standard that God sets is too high for us to achieve in our imperfect and sinful state. In Matthew 22:36 the religious leaders of the day came to Jesus to see what standard of "goodness" was good enough. They asked him, "Teacher, which is the greatest commandment in the Law?" Jesus' reply would have caught them off guard. They had always been taught to live up to a long list of rules and Jesus responds with a summary of God's standards in two quick statements. He said in Matthew 22:37-40, "Love the Lord your God with all your heart and with all your soul and with all your mind. This is the first and greatest commandment. And the second is like it: Love your neighbor as yourself. All the Law and the Prophets hang on these two commandments." If God's standard is for us to love Him and love others with everything that we are, how could we ever live up to that? If our hearts are sinful, there is nothing we could do to ever perfectly love

God and perfectly love others. Can we always keep ourselves from getting angry with someone over something insignificant, from gossiping about that annoying person we work with, from making ourselves sound important, from saying hurtful things, etc.?

When we try to live our lives doing constant good works to earn a pass with God, we become what Jesus would call "Whitewashed Tombs." In Matthew 23:27, Jesus says, "Woe to you, teachers of the law and Pharisees, you hypocrites! You are like whitewashed tombs, which look beautiful on the outside but on the inside are full of the bones of the dead and everything unclean." As a pastor, I see people living like this all the time. They want to love their kids well. They want to be nice and be part of causes that do something nice for other people. They try to help their neighbors out. But even though the outside might look good, they still do not have complete peace or total joy or completely unselfish love.

Now, I understand that in a world full of self-help books, therapy, and development plans it would be hard to believe that you can't fix yourself. Everywhere you look in our world, people are under the delusion that we can fix ourselves. Sometimes people can even find some sort of success in one part of their life, but I promise you that the underlying sinfulness in your heart can't be dealt with by any self-help book, therapy, or plan of any sort. The only way to deal with our sinful hearts is to bring it to God and become broken to have a new heart.

HOW DO I BECOME BROKEN TO HAVE A NEW HEART?

The hope that we have is that God does promise to give

us a new heart if we are willing to ask Him. This is why Jesus came, which is what we will talk about more in the next chapter. But before we learn about God's grace we must first become broken. It sounds strange because brokenness sounds like a bad thing, but it is the only path to finding healing. What I mean by brokenness is coming to a point of desperation realizing that the sin inside of you needs to be dealt with. Remember, the root of sin within us is unbelief in God and belief in ourselves to rule our life. If we truly want God to give us a new heart, then we need to come to the end of ourselves. We need to truly acknowledge that we can't save ourselves and need help. I sat with a friend several years ago that was into drugs, sex, alcohol, the whole bit. It took him coming to a point of brokenness and desperation before he was willing to let go of control and let God provide healing for him. And even if your situation is not as dire as his, your pathway is still the same. If you want to find healing, you must be willing to be desperate for God to change you.

The problem is that many times, like it says in Matthew 13:15, our hearts are calloused and hard and we don't want to change. Recently, we bought a house and in the midst of a whole host of renovations, I worked with different kinds of glues and concrete. They would harden quickly and if they ended up in the wrong spot or they didn't look the way I wanted it, I would only have one option. I would have to take something heavy, break it up, and start all over again. In our case, we don't want to go through the pain of having a broken heart. We would rather stay in our mess than deal with the pain and process of surrendering our own control. But if you want to know God and find healing, being broken before God is the only way.

So are you willing to be broken to have a new heart? If you

are, you must respond like King David did when he was confronted with his need for a new heart. King David was one of the greatest kings in Israel's history and the one to whom all other kings were compared. He had killed the giant Goliath, had been a mighty warrior, and was described as a man after God's own heart. Yet, one day he was tempted to lust after a woman named Bathsheba. He had her brought to him, got her pregnant, and then ultimately had her husband killed. After he had done this, he ignored the fact that this sinfulness was inside of him and tried to go on like everything was fine. Finally, the prophet Nathan confronted him about the sin.

Now, David could have responded like some of us do when we are confronted with our sinfulness. He could have ignored it or responded to Nathan in anger or blamed someone else for his sinfulness. Instead, he responds with a willingness to be broken to have a new heart. Psalm 51:1-5 records his response during this time period:

Have mercy on me, O God, according to your unfailing love;
according to your great compassion blot out my transgressions.
Wash away all my iniquity and cleanse me from my sin.
For I know my transgressions, and my sin is always before me.
Against you, you only, have I sinned and done what is evil in your
sight; so you are right in your verdict and justified when you judge.
Surely I was sinful at birth, sinful from the time my mother conceived
me.

He is not responding with a rote religious response or lackadaisical words. He is responding in desperation and brokenness to the reality that he is sinful and needs a new heart. There are a couple of key things he does that I think we must do if we choose to be broken to have a new heart:

1. Be willing to honestly examine your heart.

When he is crying out to God in response to His sin, he is not confessing vague ideas. He responds with very personal words because he had been confronted with the fact that sin wasn't just something out there in other people. It was something that was inside of him. When he confessed to God, he doesn't say "Have mercy on us" or "blot out the transgressions of the world" or "wash away iniquity in the world" or "cleanse the world from sin." He says, "Have mercy on *me*...blot out *my* transgressions...wash away *my* iniquity...cleanse *me* from *my* sin." He even goes so far as to say, "For I know my transgressions, and my sin is always before me." He had examined his heart and realized he hadn't just done some bad things in his life that he could correct over time. He came face to face with the reality of who he was and he wasn't happy with what he saw. He realized that his heart was full of sin and he had a desperate need for God if he was to be saved from it.

Many of us are dissatisfied with the way life is and we might even like the idea of God. We might like what we've heard about His love and might even acknowledge that God could help us have a better life. But God isn't interested in being an add-on in our lives to give us better lives. God rightfully desires all of us because He created us and He knows we are only able to honor Him and live a righteous life if He gives us a completely new heart. However, we have to be willing to be honest with ourselves and with Him before He can do anything. Unfortunately, too often we are unwilling to truly examine our hearts and understand that we far more broken than we realized. We are far too quick to think that some of our righteous deeds outweigh any sin we might have.

I have found one of the greatest ways to examine my heart is to give myself something with which to compare it. God gave us several lists in the Bible that show the kind of life that He desires for us to live. Below, I will give three of these lists and I encourage you to use them to honestly evaluate yourself and your need for God.

Ten Commandments

The Ten Commandments were God's foundational commandments to the Israelite people in the Old Testament. They are the very basics of morality. In the Gospels, Jesus takes the Ten Commandments to a new level, pointing out that even if we don't perform the acts of sin themselves, they can still be in our motivations. I have summarized the Ten Commandment principles into questions:

1. Do you have anything you worship in your life other than God?
2. Do you depend on your own knowledge and strength instead of trusting God?
3. Do you live a hypocritical life?
4. Do you set aside time in your life to honor God and rest in Him?
5. Do you honor your father and mother and those in authority over you?
6. Do you get angry with people around you?
7. Have you ever lusted after someone?
8. Have you ever taken what is not yours to take?
9. Have you ever lied or used your words to hurt other people?
10. Have you ever coveted what others around you have?

The Love Chapter

The Bible tells us that God is love and He desires for us to be filled with His love. In 1 Corinthians 13, the apostle Paul gives us a summary of what love looks like. I have written it below, but replaced the word "love" with a blank. I encourage you to insert your name into this paragraph and assess whether you are really living a life full of love:

_____ is patient,
_____ is kind.
_____ does not envy,
_____ does not boast,
_____ is not proud.
_____ does not dishonor others,
_____ is not self-seeking,
_____ is not easily angered,
_____ keeps no record of wrongs.
_____ does not delight in evil but
rejoices with the truth.
_____ always protects,
_____ always trusts,
_____ always hopes,
_____ always perseveres.

The Fruit of the Spirit

In Galatians 5:19-23 (MSG), we find a list that God identifies as sin that brings about destruction and then a list of what is called the fruit of the Spirit. The fruit of the Spirit are things that God promises to bring about in our life if we surrender our lives to Him. Which of these lists better describes your life?

Acts of the Flesh	Fruit of the Spirit
<ul><li>Repetitive, cheap sex</li><li>A stinking accumulation of mental and emotional garbage</li><li>Frenzied and joyless grabs for happiness</li><li>Trinket gods</li><li>Magic-show religion</li><li>Paranoid loneliness</li><li>Cutthroat competition</li><li>All-consuming-yet-never-satisfied wants</li><li>A brutal temper</li><li>An impotence to love or be loved</li><li>Divided homes and divided lives</li><li>Small-minded and lopsided pursuits</li><li>The vicious habit of making everyone into a rival</li><li>Uncontrolled addictions</li><li>Ugly parodies of community</li></ul>	<ul><li>Affection for others</li><li>Exuberance about life</li><li>Serenity</li><li>Willingness to stick with things</li><li>A sense of compassion in the heart</li><li>A conviction that a basic holiness permeates things and people</li><li>Has loyal commitments</li><li>Not needing to force our way in life</li><li>Able to marshal and direct our energies wisely</li></ul>

Now, there are two things we must not do with these three lists. First, we must not try to rationalize away most of the things on the list and try to reason how we could look like most of them. None of us could perfectly live out the good things on these lists, yet this is the standard that God has set for us. The point of assessing our lives like this is to help us come to the point of acknowledging that God's desire is for us to look like these lists and we are unable to do that on our own.

Second, though, we must not go the other way and tell ourselves that there is no hope for us because we could never live up to these ideals. Some of us might tell ourselves we shouldn't even pursue God because He would never accept someone who has done the bad things that we've done. We will talk more in the next chapter about how much God loves us and what He has done to bring about healing for all of us no matter who we are or what we've done. But for now, these assessments are simply to put us in a place like David where we can examine our hearts and acknowledge our sin in a personal way. This is the first step to brokenness.

2.   Acknowledge Your Sin to God.

It doesn't help us if we simply examine our sinful hearts, but never do anything about it. Part of the brokenness process is to acknowledge that sin to God. We talked in the first chapter about prayer. You may have been practicing talking to God, even if you're not sure He is really there. Now, if you really are broken to have a new heart I encourage you to acknowledge your brokenness to God. David says in Psalm 51, "Against you, you only, have I sinned and done what is evil in your sight; so you are right in your verdict and justified when you judge. Surely I was sinful at birth, sinful from the time my mother conceived me." He acknowledges His sin to God. David doesn't skirt around the issue or try to justify Himself. He tells God that He is a sinner in need of grace and He affirms that God's ways are right. And he exclaims in Psalm 51:17, "My sacrifice, O God, is a broken spirit; a broken and contrite heart you, God, will not despise."

If you asked someone who has come to saving faith in Jesus Christ, you would find that he or she had a moment where they confessed their need for God. They might not have even realized all of what they were saying. All they knew was that the life they were living was wrong and they knew that God had the answers that would fulfill them. They acknowledged how broken their life was and that they weren't following His ways. If you have never done this in your life, then I encourage you to take this step.

3.   Acknowledge Your Need to Others.

A couple years ago I was playing sand volleyball with some friends. Around the outside of the playing area was a wood border that helped to contain the sand from getting into the grass. I am pretty competitive when I play sports so I went to dive for a ball and as I did the bottom of my big toe came down on the sharp edge of that wood border. I felt pain but I didn't know what happened. As I sat on the ground and looked down at my toe I realized that there was a giant gash where the skin of my big toe had been pulled back. It was pretty gruesome. Now, if I had recognized that my toe was like that but decided to just let it go and get back into the game, people would have thought I was crazy. Or if I had refused any help and tried to deal with it myself, I would have risked greater injury, infection, and other troubles. But isn't this what we do sometimes when we are confronted with our need? We try to hide it from other people and deal with it ourselves.

If you have truly recognized your need for God (that might be as gruesome as my injured toe) and have acknowledged that need to God, then I have found that another important step in the journey of brokenness is to ask others for help. Thankfully, when I hurt my toe I had a friend who was willing to take several hours to help me to a car, take me to a doctor's office, and wait with me to get help. And I know there are countless Bible-believing Christians who would be honored to help you take the next step in knowing God, but you have to be willing to acknowledge your need to them. Hopefully, you are doing this study with someone who knows God personally, but if not then I encourage you to find someone who knows God and who you can trust with your brokenness. Tell them your story of brokenness and ask them if they would be willing to help you on your journey. You might be scared to share some of these things with another person, but I promise you that if you are willing to be honest with God and honest with others there will be a huge weight lifted off your shoulders.

If you are reading this and you have already come to know God, I would still encourage you to not miss out on the opportunity to be broken to have a new heart. We never stop needing to be broken. Actually, the more we come to know God the more broken we should become because we should be continually humbled by who God is as we learn more about Him. So, maybe it has been a while since you have examined your own heart, acknowledged your sin to God, and acknowledged your need to others. James 5:16 says, "Therefore, confess your sins to each other and pray for each other so that you may be healed. The prayer of a righteous man is powerful and effective." We need to be willing to continue to engage in brokenness as we walk out our life of faith.

So, we have discovered the second step of knowing God, becoming broken to have a new heart. It takes us being willing to examine our hearts, acknowledge our sin to God, and acknowledge our need to others. This might seem like a difficult step and it is messy, but in the next chapter we will learn about the beauty that God wants to bring out of this brokenness.

REFLECTION QUESTIONS

1. After reading this chapter, how would you define "heart" and "sin" differently than you may have in the past?
2. Sin is the curving of the soul inward, where we trust ourselves instead of trusting God. One of the effects of sin is that it is terribly deceptive. How have you seen this deception in your life?
3. An important element of understanding the heart and sin is understanding that sin is not just something we do…it is something in our very nature. The actions of young children were used as examples of this reality. Do you believe this? Do you think this contradicts what our society believes?
4. Death and decay are the result of sin. We see the evidence of this all around. In us, sin is the cause of physical death, spiritual death, and eternal death if we do not choose to accept Jesus. Yet, we often try to blame death and decay in our lives on things other than sin. Why do you think we do this?

5. Many of us think we can get ourselves out of the situation by doing good things or being a better person. We talked about how this is impossible because sin even corrupts the good things we do and God's standard is perfection which we cannot reach on our own. Why do you think this is hard for us to accept?

6. In order to receive a new heart, we have to be broken (or desperate) for God to work in our lives. When is the last time you were desperate for something and what did your desperation look like?

7. Which one of the application steps below will be most difficult for you?

APPLICATION

1. Be willing to honestly examine your own heart – Take time to work through the questions included in this section of the chapter and seek to discover an honest assessment of yourself before God.

2. Acknowledge your sin to God – Take time to pray and acknowledge that you have a sinful heart and are in need of God's help. Ask God to help you see yourself through His eyes.

3. Acknowledge your need for others – Take some time to talk to someone else about what you are reading in this chapter. Confess the brokenness you see in yourself and ask them if they could walk with you in your journey of knowing God.

Step 3
SURRENDERED TO GOD'S GRACE

When we would reminisce about old family stories growing up, my parents would always tell this one story about my sister. She was a strong-willed child growing up and my parents said they could see it even before she was two years old. This one day she took keys that she wasn't supposed to take and threw them on the ground with that look of defiance little kids get. My mom took her over to the keys and asked her to pick them up. She stood her ground and with some attitude refused to pick up the keys. My sister was told that she would wait there and not be able to play with her toys until she listened and was obedient. Five minutes went by, then ten, then twenty, and so on until it had been forty-five minutes. Finally, with a look of disgust my sister finally gave up, picked up the keys, and gave them back to my mom. She realized in her little mind that nothing was going to change unless she was willing to surrender.

Up until this point in our discussion about knowing God, we have focused on some of the preparation that has to be done in our hearts to be ready to know God. In this chapter we finally come to the point of decision of whether we want to start a relationship with God or not. Many words have been used to describe this decision but I can't think of a more applicable term than "surrender." It just might not be the kind of surrender that you're thinking of. In that moment of surrender for my sister, she was frustrated and angry and didn't want to surrender because she wanted to do her own thing. Surrender to God may look like this in some of our lives, where we are brought kicking and screaming to the realization that we have ignored His love and care for us long enough. However, surrender doesn't always have to be to something that we don't desire. Sometimes, the most powerful surrender is when we surrender to the thing that we have always wanted and desired, just did not think we deserved. The important part is to realize that no matter how we surrender, it always results in trading in our way of doing things for another's. If you have truly come to the point of being humbled and broken, this may be the kind of battle that is going on in your own heart. You may be feeling that gentle tug in the direction of God's will. Maybe you are not quite there yet. Whatever the case, if you want to know God, surrender is the only option.

I hope in this chapter to explain to you in the most descriptive way possible how amazing the grace of God is for each one of us. The simple call to each one of us at the end will be, "Are you willing to surrender to God's grace?"

WHAT IS GRACE?

In order to understand the amazing grace of God, we must first start with understanding what grace really means. Grace is a term that is rarely used in our society. One of the only examples I could think of is receiving a grace period for loans. If you have any kind of student debt in particular, there are usually a couple months after your education when you are given a reprieve from paying back your debt. You didn't deserve that time and didn't do anything to earn that time. It is given freely as a chance for you to catch up after your education.[11]

This is not a perfect example, but it points in the direction of a biblical definition for grace. Several key elements have to be met if something is to be considered grace.[12] First, it must be free and freely attained, meaning it is without strings attached and anyone can have access to it. In our church, a statement we use to describe this reality of grace is "No matter who you are or what you've done." God's grace is open to absolutely anyone and there are no barriers to someone receiving it if they choose to surrender to Him.

A second key element of grace is that it is undeserved, meaning that the person receiving grace does not deserve what is given. Grace is not something that we can earn in our own strength. By it's very definition, grace is given to those that can't deserve it. And the more undeserving someone is, the more they cherish the grace they've been given. Jesus tells a parable in Luke 7:41-42 about two people that owed a certain amount of money to a moneylender. One owed five hundred and the other fifty. Jesus says, "Neither of them had the money to pay him back, so he forgot the debts of both. Now which of them will love him more?" Both people were given grace and both should have appreciated it, but the one who had more of a debt was understandably more appreciative. The greater point of this parable is that no matter who we are, we are all undeserving of God's grace and can't do anything to earn it.

The final key element of grace is that it not only pardons freely, but it actually produces favor in someone's life: meaning the person is given rights and privileges they don't deserve. In terms of God's grace, we are described in the Bible as rebellious in our sin and turning away from our privileges as sons and daughters of God. Yet when we choose to surrender to God's grace, He bestows His favor on us by giving us all the rights and privileges of His children. Jesus gives a famous parable to describe this in Luke 15 called the parable of the prodigal son. He tells of a man that had two sons. The younger of the two sons came to him and asked him for the share of the estate that he was supposed to receive when his father died. The son then proceeded to take all he had and run away to a far away land, squandering all his wealth on momentary pleasures and "wild living." The money ran out, his friends abandoned him, a famine struck the land, and he was forced to work for a pig farmer simply to survive. He was so hungry at times that he yearned to eat what the pigs were eating. After a time, he came to the decision that he would go back to his father, confess his sin, and ask his father to make him a hired hand so at least he would not starve.

After what he had done, he would never have dreamed he could go back to having the rights and privileges of being a "son." And yet in this amazing statement in Luke 15:20 it says, "But while he was still a long way off, his father saw him and was filled with compassion for him; he ran to his son, threw his arms around him and kissed him." And as the son confesses his sin and makes his plea, it says in Luke 15:22-24, "But the father said to his servants, 'Quick! Bring the best robe and put it on him. Put a ring on his finger and sandals on his feet. Bring the fattened calf and kill it. Let's have a feast and celebrate. For this son of mine was dead and is alive again; he was lost and is found.' So they began to celebrate." In that culture it was very unusual for a father to express his love in this way. It was extravagant. We might think it fair for the father to receive him back as a farmhand, but I doubt we would think that the son deserved this type of welcome from his father. Yet the father willingly bestows his favor on his son even though he didn't deserve it.

God's grace is given to us in a similar fashion if we are willing to surrender to Him. If, like the son in the parable, we are broken enough to realize our need for Him and we come to Him in surrender to what He wants for us, He does not just forgive our debt. He clothes us in His righteousness, He gives us a new identity, He pours His love into our lives, and throws a party in heaven. We don't deserve any of this, but His grace is that amazing.

THE CROSS AND GRACE

You might say, "Okay, I think I understand that God's grace is free, undeserved, and gives favor to us, but why do I need God's grace and how do I have access to it?" In the last chapter, we talked extensively about our need for a New Heart because of sin and this is why we are in need of God's grace. Without God's grace, we are still stuck in our sin and we can't do anything to change that. In fact, as we talked about in the last chapter, our hearts are not just broken. They are dead. Ephesians 2:1-2 says, "As for you, you were dead in your transgressions and sins, in which you used to live when you followed the ways of this world and of the ruler of the kingdom of the air, the spirit who is now at work in those who are disobedient." Our situation is not that we are bad people that need to be made better; we are dead people that need to be made alive. We are by our very nature rebels against God. Ephesians 2 continues by saying, "All of us also lived among them at one time, gratifying the cravings of our flesh and following its desires and thoughts. Like the rest, we were by nature deserving of wrath." According to United States Law, someone convicted of treason can be given the death penalty, because that person has been found to be a rebel to the laws of our country. Our sinful position as rebels puts us in the place of deserving God's wrath because we have turned our back on Him.

And unfortunately, this rebellious position does something worse than just a physical death. According to the Bible, God chooses to not violate our free will because that would make us like robots instead of loved sons and daughters. So if we choose to be in rebellion against Him, He will not force us to be with Him. What this means practically is that the punishment and wrath we receive for denying God is to spend eternity in separation from Him in Hell. The Bible repeatedly says God wants all of us to be with Him in Heaven for all of eternity, but He won't force us. So we must understand that our choice of whether to surrender to God's grace or not is the most important decision that we can make in life. In fact, it is the most important decision that anyone can make. It has eternal ramifications.

Even if we understand why we need God's grace, how do we have access to it? Grace is freely given, but that doesn't mean it comes without a cost. If we believe God to be who the Bible claims Him to be, He is the perfect, all-knowing, all-powerful, loving and compassionate Creator of the universe. His perfect nature entails that He cannot be associated with sin because it is in His nature to bring about justice. In fact, in the Old Testament there had to be a sacrifice in order for someone to meet with God freely. Again, put it in the context of a court of justice where someone needs his or her debt forgiven. The judge stands as one who must bring about justice and if the person cannot fulfill his or her obligations, then someone else must pay for the debt. Otherwise, punishment must be dealt out to the one owes the debt. In the same way, certain sacrifices in the Old Testament received the punishment that should have come upon the people in order for them to come into the presence of God. The priest would make these sacrifices on behalf of everyone, including himself. This is described in Hebrews 5:1-3, "Every high priest is selected from among the people and is appointed to represent the people in matters related to God, to offer gifts and sacrifices for sins. He is able to deal gently with those who are ignorant and are going astray, since he himself is subject to weakness. This is why he has to offer sacrifices for his own sins, as well as for the sins of the people." This is how things were for a long time.

Unfortunately, these sacrifices did not deal with the problem at its root. They were temporary and only dealt with the consequences of sin, not with the heart of sin itself. In the Old Testament, there are promises that God, in due time, would bring about a final solution to the problem of sin within our hearts. This is where Jesus and the cross come in. If the very heart of sin was to be dealt with, then there had to be someone who could perfectly live out the commands of God and then willingly sacrifice their life for the atonement of sins once and for all. And if this person was to bring life and freedom, then they needed to be able to conquer sin and death. The problem with this is the only person that qualified for that job would be God Himself. He was the only one who could perfectly live out a righteous life. He was the only one who could conquer sin and death.

So God chose to do something extraordinary, even unfathomable. Galatians 4:4 describes it well: "But when the time had fully come, God sent His Son, born of a woman, born under law, to redeem those under law, that we might receive the full rights of sons." It's also described in Romans 5:6-8, "You see, at just the right time, when we were still powerless, Christ died for the ungodly. Very rarely will anyone die for a righteous man, though for a good man someone might possibly dare to die. But God demonstrates his own love for us in this: while we were still sinners, Christ died for us." While we were still powerless in our sin, condemned and unable to freely be in the presence of God, God sent His Son, Jesus Christ, as the final sacrifice for sin.

You might ask why Jesus qualified to be the sacrifice for our sins? Jesus is the central figure of all of history. Read what was said about him in the Nicene Creed, a creed of the early church:

I believe in one Lord Jesus Christ, the Only Begotten Son of God,
born of the Father before all ages.
God from God, Light from Light, true God from true God,
begotten, not made, consubstantial with the Father;
through him all things were made.
For us men and for our salvation he came down from heaven,
and by the Holy Spirit was incarnate of the Virgin Mary,
and became man.

For our sake he was crucified under Pontius Pilate,
he suffered death and was buried, and rose again on the third day
in accordance with the Scriptures.
He ascended into heaven and is seated at the right hand of the Father.
He will come again in glory to judge the living and the dead
and his kingdom will have no end.[13]

It would take several chapters to fully understand what this creed is saying, but here is a summary of what was so important about Jesus. Jesus was fully God and yet chose to become man. He was involved in the creation of the world and yet chose to become part of that creation to save us. Jesus was born of a virgin as was necessary, since according to Scripture sin was passed down through the male. He was born without a sinful nature, lived a perfect life, and when the time came He willingly gave up His life to die as the final sacrifice for our sins. But if this were where it ended, He would have only been an amazing person with the big claim of having taken care of our sin. There would have probably been a religion started about Him that would be like all of the other religions whose chief figures are still in the grave. But this was different. Jesus backed up His claims with the most improbable of actions. After being buried for three days, He rose again from the dead.

I saw an article recently about sports figures who made claims and then backed them up.[14] One of the most famous examples was the quarterback Joe Namath. He was the quarterback of the New York Jets and they were to face the Baltimore Colts in the championship game. The Jets were part of the American Football League and an AFL team had never won the championship game. Nonetheless, Namath came out before the game and without even full confidence from his coach he guaranteed that they would win the championship.[15] To everyone's amazement, they did end up beating the Colts in the championship game with a score of 16-7. Namath became a legend because it is so rare to make a great claim and follow-through on it.

Jesus did something even more extraordinary. He claimed to be God Himself. The religious teachers of the day hated Him because they knew He was claiming to be something more than just a teacher. He made it clear that He was God by claiming to be one with God the Father (John 10:30). This was an outrageous claim to a first century Jewish person and a pretty big claim today as well. How many times have we heard of someone who is insane claiming to be a deity? It causes us to be skeptical of claims like this. Yet, Jesus' situation was different. C.S. Lewis points out in his famous book "Mere Christianity" that the most probable solution is that Jesus really is God:

I am trying here to prevent anyone saying the really foolish thing that people often say about Him: I'm ready to accept Jesus as a great moral teacher, but I don't accept his claim to be God. That is the one thing we must not say. A man who was merely a man and said the sort of things Jesus said would not be a great moral teacher. He would either be a lunatic—on the level with the man who says he is a poached egg—or else he would be the Devil of Hell. You must make your choice. Either this man was, and is, the Son of God, or else a madman or something worse. You can shut him up for a fool, you can spit at him and kill him as a demon or you can fall at his feet and call him Lord and God, but let us not come with any patronising nonsense about his being a great human teacher. He has not left that open to us. He did not intend to. . . . Now it seems to me obvious that He was neither a lunatic nor a fiend: and consequently, however strange or terrifying or unlikely it may seem, I have to accept the view that He was and is God.[16]

If you remotely believe that the Bible is true (and there is great evidence to believe this), then you would at least have to acknowledge Jesus was a great moral teacher. People have approved of many of His teachings as loving and beneficial to society whether they are believers or not. It doesn't sound like the ramblings of a lunatic. Lewis demonstrates in this passage that if you take all of Jesus' claims into account, then there are only three options for Jesus: He is a liar, lunatic, or our Lord. The question we must ask ourselves is, how could a man that did such amazing things for people and who taught such amazing truths be a liar or a lunatic? I agree with Lewis, that Jesus' claims about being God make the most sense.

The other claim He made was that He would be raised from the dead after His crucifixion. He tried to tell His disciples this before His death but they didn't really understand what He was saying to them at the time (Mark 8:31, John 2:19, Matthew 27:63). In some ways, this claim is just as big as His claim of being God since there had never been anyone before in the history of the world that in their own power defeated death. Being resurrected seems like an impossibility to those who have never seen it.

Yet, the resurrection stands out as such a strong historical fact that it is hard to discount. Dr. Craig Hazen is a renowned scholar in the area of evidence for the resurrection. We as a church had the privilege of hosting a conference with Dr. Hazen as the keynote speaker. He took a historical approach to the resurrection and identified twelve historical facts surrounding the resurrection with which most scholars (whether they were believers or not) would not disagree. He then uses those historical facts to test every theory that has ever been put forth to explain away the resurrection. It was a fascinating discussion. In the end, Dr. Hazen finds there are only two explanations that fit all of the criteria: either Jesus was resurrected or He was an alien.[17] I don't know about you, but it would be hard for me to believe in aliens in general, let alone that Jesus was an alien. His point in all of this is that even though other people might try to downplay the reality of the resurrection it is the most historically probable possibility when you take all of the known facts into consideration. If you have more questions about whether the resurrection really happened, I will include some of Craig Hazen's material and other scholars' work on the topic at the end of the chapter.

The main point to take away from all of this is that if Jesus was raised from the dead, it changes everything. The apostle Paul says as much in 1 Corinthians 15:12-22:

> *But if it is preached that Christ has been raised from the dead, how can some of you say that there is no resurrection of the dead? If there is no resurrection of the dead, then not even Christ has been raised. And if Christ has not been raised, our preaching is useless and so is your faith. More than that, we are then found to be false witnesses about God, for we have testified about God that he raised Christ from the dead. But he did not raise him if in fact the dead are not raised. For if the dead are not raised, then Christ has not been raised either. And if Christ has not been raised, your faith is futile; you are still in your sins. Then those also who have fallen asleep in Christ are lost. If only for this life we have hope in Christ, we are of all people most to be pitied. But Christ has indeed been raised from the dead, the firstfruits of those who have fallen asleep. For since death came through a man, the resurrection of the dead comes also through a man. For as in Adam all die, so in Christ all will be made alive.*

Paul argues that our entire faith rests on the resurrection of Jesus. He explains that if Jesus has not been raised from the dead, then we have no hope to deal with our sinful hearts. We are stuck in our pain and emptiness. But he affirms that if Jesus did in fact rise from the dead, then we can have hope to conquer the sin that came through Adam and Eve at the beginning.

Hopefully it has become apparent how desperately we need the grace of God. Someone needs to pay for the sinfulness in our hearts and we are unable to pay that price. We have access to God's grace because of Jesus' death and resurrection. His death pays the penalty for our sin and His resurrection conquers the death that comes with sin. However, even if you understand this as a general idea, you might wonder whether God will give His grace to you personally? You might look at the things you have done throughout your life (even the things that no one else knows about) and wonder how God could really forgive you.

HIS GREAT LOVE

Ephesians 2:4-10 is a wonderful passage describing surrender and the grace of God. In the passage, we get a clear idea of why God would choose to do something this amazing for us:

But because of his great love for us, God, who is rich in mercy, made us alive with Christ even when we were dead in transgressions—it is by grace you have been saved. And God raised us up with Christ and seated us with him in the heavenly realms in Christ Jesus, in order that in the coming ages he might show the incomparable riches of his grace, expressed in his kindness to us in Christ Jesus. For it is by grace you have been saved, through faith—and this is not from yourselves, it is the gift of God— not by works, so that no one can boast. For we are God's handiwork, created in Christ Jesus to do good works, which God prepared in advance for us to do.

There is a phrase repeated continually in Ephesians 2: "it is by grace you have been saved." God the Father sent Jesus "because of His great love for us" and because He is "rich in mercy." Remember when we talked about the Prodigal Son earlier in the chapter? God is like that Father, willing and waiting to give us His grace. And He doesn't need us to get all cleaned up before we accept His grace. The passage says God "made us alive with Christ even when we were dead in our transgressions."

Our son just turned three years old and we are so grateful for him. I had never really taken care of kids before we had our son, so the idea of changing diapers, dealing with snotty noses, and cleaning up messes worried me. I was always grossed out by that stuff when I was with other peoples' kids. The strange thing is, when you become a parent all of that doesn't seem as big of a deal. You just love your child so much that it is a part of life. And as Judah gets older, the messes in his life won't be about snotty noses anymore, but instead it will be about how to navigate mistakes he's made and problems in which he finds himself. I know that as a father, the last thing I would want my son to do would be to run away from me in those times because he feels like he needs to fix his problems before he comes to me. If even I, a mere man, have that kind of love for my son, imagine the love that God has for us. He loves us so much. He doesn't care that we are broken and messy. All He wants is for us to surrender to His love and the grace He has for us. So if you feel like you don't deserve

God's grace, you are in good company. None of us do and that is the whole point.

So far we have figured out why we need God's grace and we have talked about how it is possible. We can have access to God's grace because of Jesus' death and resurrection, and God is calling us to surrender to the grace He demonstrated by Jesus' sacrifice. How do we actually surrender to His grace though?

HOW DO I SURRENDER TO GOD'S GRACE?

There are two important pieces to understand if we want to surrender to God's grace: faith and repentance.

1.   Surrendering to God's grace involves faith.

Ephesians 2:8-9 says, "For it is by grace you have been saved, through faith." God never calls us to a blind faith. The faith that God talks about in the Bible is a reasonable certainty. He asks us to consider all of the things we know and take a step of faith based on that. For instance, if you have ever been part of a leadership group or a team training, you may have done something called a "trust fall." I was a resident assistant in college and we went for a team training once where he had to do a "trust fall." A person stands backwards on a raised platform and gets in a position to fall off the platform. The other people stand below and when everything is ready someone makes the call for the person to fall without knowing if the people are going to catch them. It is meant to develop team trust. But imagine someone asked you to do a trust fall without knowing the people that were going to catch you. That is blind faith (and to me it is kind of crazy). If I don't know anything about these people, how do I expect them to catch me? God doesn't expect us to surrender to Him without knowing anything about Him. He calls us to surrender based on what we know about Him.

On the other hand, even if you're doing a "trust fall" with people you know, it still takes faith to fall. You can't see with your eyes whether the people are going to catch you. It goes against everything in you to give up your own control and fall backwards depending completely on someone else. In the same way, you might say, "How am I supposed to know He is really there if I cannot see Him with my own eyes? How do I know I am not just praying to the ceiling?" That is where faith comes in. Based on what you know about God, are you willing to fall, trusting that He will catch you?

I have watched many people get stuck at this very point and refuse to surrender to God's grace. Many people that would even consider themselves Christians are stuck at this point: reaching back to fall into God's arms while still desperately clinging to the platform. You can study God for your entire life and still never be satisfied enough to surrender, just like you could study the personal lives of every person that was going to catch you in a "trust fall," study the aerodynamics of falling, study the psychological perceptions of team bonding, study the fear of falling and how it can be defeated, and none of it would ever matter if you didn't actually trust your team enough to fall. Maybe you still have some nagging doubts about a particular question about God or a life situation. By all means search out someone who might have an answer for you, but the reality is that we will always have more questions. God and His grace are beyond our full comprehension. How small of a God would He be if we could fully understand Him? Maybe you have even studied the Bible, gone to church, been baptized, taken communion faithfully, done many good deeds, and still have never really surrendered to the amazing grace of God because you are afraid to fully give up control.

Whatever the case, surrender takes faith. Actually, faith is defined by surrender. Surrender takes a willingness to be dependent on someone else. In a society like ours where so many things are about us being independent and taking control of our own lives it can be so hard for people to truly surrender to God's grace. But it is our only hope. Jesus said in John 14:6, "I am the way and the truth and the life. No one comes to the Father except through me." The faith steps we must take if we are to surrender to God's grace are first to believe that Jesus' death and resurrection are true and sufficient to save us from our sins. Then, we must confess that we are willing to let Jesus take control of your heart now. In Romans 10:9-10 it says, "If you declare with your mouth, 'Jesus is Lord,' and believe in your heart that God raised him from the dead, you will be saved. For it is with your heart that you believe and are justified, and it is with your mouth that you profess your faith and are saved." It is as simple as sincerely declaring from your heart that you believe Jesus is who He said He is and that you are now willing to let Him take control of your life.

2. Surrendering to God's grace involves Repentance.

The other important part of surrendering to God's grace is understanding you didn't receive this grace based on your own merits. Again, Ephesians 2:8-9 says, "For it is by grace you have been saved through faith – and this not from yourselves, it is the gift of God – not by works, so that no one can boast." God's grace is a gift. A gift ceases to be a gift when someone believes they've earned it. This past Christmas my wife got me new headphones. If my wife gave me the box they were in and I had opened it and said, "Great, these are exactly what I deserved" what do you think she would have done? Knowing how sweet she is, she probably would have been disappointed but still let me keep them. Most people, including myself, though, would probably grab the box and take them back to the store. Why? Because if someone receiving a gift thinks they deserve it, then they misunderstand their condition and the nature of a gift. In the last chapter and earlier in this chapter, we demonstrated that we don't deserve anything from God. We are the broken and rebellious ones who are dead in our trespasses and sins. We have run away from God. We don't have the ability to be perfect in God's sight. And God doesn't have an obligation to forgive us. This is what makes His grace through Jesus's death and resurrection so powerful. He didn't have to do it. Yet, because of His great love, He chose to give us the gift of redemption.

This is why surrendering to God's grace involves something called repentance. In the book of Acts, when the apostle Peter is preaching, the people ask him about how to surrender to God's grace. He says in Acts 2:38, "Repent and be baptized, every one of you, in the name of the Lord Christ for the forgiveness of your sins." Repentance is being willing to turn your back on your former way of life in order to turn toward Christ. It is your willingness to declare that all the works you have done up to this point have accomplished nothing to get you close to God and you are willing to forsake them all in order to follow Him.

ARE YOU READY?

Are you ready to surrender to God's grace? If so, it is as

simple as praying a prayer of surrender based on what we have been talking about with faith and repentance in your heart. Here is an example of what a prayer of surrender might look like:

Father God, I have been humbled by the fact that you are God and I am not. I am broken, recognizing that I am sinful and in need of a new heart. I believe in my heart that Jesus is who He said He is, that He died on the cross for my sins and was raised from the dead, conquering sin and death forever. I repent of my own way of doing things, recognizing that my own works have gotten me nowhere. I surrender to Your grace and offer my life to You because You deserve it. I give up control and ask You to guide me from this moment forward in every thought and action. Thank You for Your grace!

Now, the words of the prayer don't matter as much as the heart behind the prayer. There are many people who claim to be Christians because they have prayed some words from a prayer at some point in their life, but their hearts are still far away from God. The prayer is simply a demonstration of a heart attitude of surrender.

If you chose to pray this prayer and truly meant it, your life will never be the same again. You have now been welcomed into the family of God. You are a Christian, and God's grace will start to permeate all of your life. You have been forgiven of your sins and God can and will do supernatural things in your life to free you from the effects of sin. This is the beginning of an amazing journey that will lead to the ultimate destination of dwelling with God for all of eternity in Heaven.

If you are still not sure whether you want to surrender to God's grace or not, consider this quote from E. Stanley Jones:

The strangest thing on this planet is our fear of surrendering to the one safe place in the universe — God. We hug our present delusions, knowing deep down that they are delusions; but they are present, and we hug them for fear of the unknown. But that unknown is love. The earth when it runs away from the sun simply runs into the dark. When we run away from God, refuse to surrender ourselves, then we get one thing — the dark.[18]

If you have more questions about God's grace, please search out some answers for those questions. But if you understand what God has done for you and you still resist because it is easier to stay where you are, then I beg you to take the step of faith to surrender to God's grace. Otherwise, all you will be doing is spending more time in the dark like the moth we talked about at the beginning of the book, instead of enjoying the blessings that God has for you.

Finally, if you already know God and have surrendered to His grace in the past, don't forget that salvation happens both in a moment and every day. Jesus said to his disciples in Luke 9:23, "Whoever wants to be my disciple must deny themselves and take up their cross daily and follow me." Do you remember on a daily basis the love shown to you through the cross and the favor you now have because of Jesus' sacrifice? It should be the foundation of everything we do in life. This is what we will discuss in the next chapters. Surrendering to God's grace is only the beginning to the journey of knowing God.

REFLECTION QUESTIONS

1. How do you define grace after reading this chapter?
2. There were different reasons given in this chapter as to

why Jesus needed to die on the Cross. Which reason made the most sense to you? Any reasons you are confused about?

3. There were also many reasons given for why we can trust Jesus and testimony about Him. One of those reasons followed the thinking of C.S. Lewis in saying that Jesus was either a liar, lunatic, or our Lord. Do you think this is a valid argument? Why or why not?

4. It is imperative that we decide whether we believe in the resurrection of Jesus or not, because if Jesus really did rise from the dead then all of the Bible's claims prove true. If someone asked you to explain whether you think the resurrection happened or not what would you say?

5. We talked about how salvation only comes to us when we are willing to acknowledge "it is by grace you have been saved" and not because of something we have done. Is it frustrating to you that we can't save ourselves?

6. We talked about the "trust fall" moment in surrendering to God's grace. God doesn't call us to completely blind faith, but we still must exercise faith if we are to surrender to Him. Many of us get to that moment and try to surrender while still holding onto our own lives, but that doesn't work. Have you had a "trust fall" moment in your life and if not, are you willing to?

7. Which of the application steps below applies to you? Is there anything standing in the way of you taking that step?

APPLICATION

1. Receive God's grace – If you have never surrendered to God's grace before then I urge you to pray the prayer included in this chapter. If you do this in faith, your life

will never be the same again.

2. Remember God's grace – If you have already received God's grace in your life, then take time to remember what God's grace has accomplished in your life. Ask yourself if there are any ways you have lost sight of God's grace in your life.

RESOURCES

Dr. Craig Hazen, *Evidence for the Resurrection of Jesus*, (Biola University, 2006).

Dr. Gary Habermas, *The Risen Jesus and Future Hope*, (New York, Rowman and Littlefield Publishers, Inc., 2003).

Dr. Gary Habermas and Michael Licona, *The Case for the Resurrection of Jesus*, (Grand Rapids: Kregel Publications, 2004).

Step 4
REVIVED FOR AUTHENTIC LIVING

Most descriptions of knowing Jesus would get to this point of the process and stop. Many people that come to a saving knowledge of Jesus Christ may have stopped at this point as well. But to experience being humbled, broken, and surrendered is not the end of our journey of knowing God. It is simply the beginning. Imagine that friend of yours who always has a crazy story. We all have that friend who is always talking about adventures he has been on and people he has met. Imagine he comes up to you one day and tells you about a famous actor he happened to meet at the airport. He would tell you how he saw the actor from afar and had to come to terms with whether it was really them or not. Then he had to overcome the nervousness of whether he would introduce himself. Finally, he would tell you about how he started a conversation with the person and what that person was like.

Now, if he were to tell you all of this, and then talk about "knowing" that person you would be a little skeptical. Right? Does he really know the actor after just having met him? The word "know" means many things in our English language. The first time you meet someone you could say that you got to know him or her. But later on after you have spent a lot of time with that person you could say you know him or her and it would mean something very different. Now, you know what he or she likes and doesn't like. You know how they act in different situations. You know what makes him or her tick. And the word "know" takes on a completely different meaning if you are married to someone. One of the biblical words for "know" can actually infer sexual intimacy between a couple. That is about as close and intimate as you can get.

For us in our journey towards knowing God, we must understand that coming to the point of starting a relationship with Jesus is only the beginning. Knowing God in our daily life, letting Him change us from the inside out, and living that out in love toward others is as essential to knowing God as first meeting Him. And the first step of knowing God in our daily life is where we find ourselves in this chapter. We have received God's grace for salvation and begun a relationship with Him. The first step of knowing Him after that experience I call being "revived for authentic living." In this chapter, I will explain what kind of life God wants us to live on a daily basis and how He revives us to live that way, as we know Him more.

WHAT IS AUTHENTIC LIVING?

Let's begin with the question of what is meant by authentic living. Well, in today's world "authentic" has become a buzzword. Hipsters, organizations, and marketing campaigns all talk about being authentic which usually entails being real and showing your faults as well as your strengths. When I say "authentic living" there are elements that overlap with this popular notion of authenticity, but what I mean is more in line with authenticating something. The real question of authentic living is asking ourselves whether the daily actions we are taking line up with claiming to know God. Is God's grace starting to shape the way we see, hear, and interact with the world around us or are we still living the same way we did before we said we knew God? Are we starting to be freed from the lies that have kept us from the life that God has wanted for us?

Authentic living is so important because if surrendering to God's grace made us feel good for a moment but didn't do anything to change our everyday life, then what is the purpose of it? God didn't save us from our sins for momentary bliss. He saved us from our sins so we could have a completely transformed life where all the darkness becomes light and all of the brokenness becomes healed. The apostle Paul says in 1 Corinthians 5:17, "Therefore, if anyone is in Christ, the new creation has come: The old has gone, the new is here!" We start to be made new in every aspect of our lives because of God's grace. It doesn't happen in an instant, but it happens as you commit to knowing God in your daily life.

Being made new probably sounds like a great thing to all of us, but the problem with being made new and living authentically like Jesus is that after we have spent our whole lives living without God's grace we can have a hard time changing. Recently, my cousin showed me a new top of the line virtual reality system he purchased. I had never experienced anything like it before. As you walk into the room there are special cameras mounted on the wall. You put on a headset and immediately you are no longer looking at the real walls of the room. Instead, you feel as though you are in whatever program the computer is running whether it be a warehouse, a bustling city, or a spaceport. You also have controllers in your hands that let you interact with the virtual world you are now seeing. You can pick things up, throw things, and walk around. It is incredible and eerily lifelike. In one program I tried, I got into an elevator and was taken to a very high floor of a skyscraper. When the elevator opened there was a plank that I was supposed to walk out. Now, I knew it wasn't real, but it was still terrifying to try to inch out onto that virtual plank. Then he told me to jump off and I almost fell over when I did because my mind was telling me that I was falling even though in real life I was not.

Now, imagine that your life before knowing God was like that virtual reality system. You were living in a world that looked real, felt real, and sounded real. You viewed yourself, the world, and everything around you in terms of your own perception. You believed the world's wisdom of what was right and wrong. But if you have surrendered to God's grace you have discovered that the life you were living was not real. It is like taking off those goggles to discover the real world around you. It is wonderful and exciting, but imagine how disorienting and overwhelming it could be at the same time. Everything you once knew was tainted by sin and death. To live authentically like Jesus, God desires to teach you a new way to live in every aspect of your life.

There are several different responses we can have to this wonderful discovery. Jesus tells a parable that I believe conveys these responses well. He says in Matthew 13:3-9:

74

A farmer went out to sow his seed. As he was scattering the seed, some fell along the path, and the birds came and ate it up. Some fell on rocky places, where it did not have much soil. It sprang up quickly, because the soil was shallow. But when the sun came up, the plants were scorched, and they withered because they had no root. Other seed fell among thorns, which grew up and choked the plants. Still other seed fell on good soil, where it produced a crop—a hundred, sixty or thirty times what was sown. Whoever has ears, let them hear.

The seed represents the Good News about Jesus and the kingdom of God. Different reactions toward what God wants to do in our lives are described in terms of the type of soil the seed finds. First, some seed might fall along the path, meaning that the person does not fully understand the Good News and the enemy steals away the joy and freedom they could have had. Second, some seed might fall on rocky soil meaning that the person understands the Good News and reacts with joy, but because there is no root it only lasts a short time. Third, some seed might fall among the thorns, meaning that the person understands the Good News and starts becoming new, but the worries of this life start to choke out what God can do in them. Finally, the person who receives the seed on good soil is described. This person does not resist the Good News and instead embraces it. An amazing crop of new life is produced in him or her.

Now, let's take this parable and put it in the context of the virtual reality goggles. Remember, we said that when we surrender to God's grace we discover a new world around us. We find out that God wants to bring us new life and cause us to live authentically, like Jesus, daily. I think some people react to this by not fully understanding it. They don't see much difference between the virtual world and the real world and so they just keep living the same way they did in the virtual world. The result of this is that they are still living in deception. They might have prayed a prayer, but they start to think that there is nothing to this "religious stuff." They start to wonder whether what they experienced was even true and ultimately turn away from God.

Others react with overwhelming joy when they first take the goggles off. They discover that the real world is more beautiful and amazing than the virtual world could have ever been. God starts to do some amazing things in their lives. What they feel, think, and do changes. The problem is, instead of continuing to pursue knowing God, they just keep living their life hoping this new way of life continues on its own. Unfortunately, when troubles come along their path, their faith is not rooted and they fall away.

Still others react by taking off the goggles and embracing what God wants to do in them. They are amazed at the real world around them and they may even pursue knowing Jesus more by going to church, reading the Bible, praying, and many other ways. Unfortunately, in the end, they are tempted to go back into the virtual world because they think it is more comfortable and doesn't ask them to change. This chokes out the authentic life that God wants to give them.

Finally, the last group of people takes off the goggles and is overwhelmed by the amazing journey on which God takes them. Every new step into the real world of God's grace is an exciting discovery of the lies they once believed and the truth God now provides. They understand following this path is not always easy and might call them into uncomfortable situations where their obedience to God is tested, but they trust what it says in Romans 8:28, "And we know that in all things God works for the good of those who love him, who have been called according to his purpose." God starts to make them new in every aspect of their life. They start to live and act like Jesus did. They start to become rooted in the truth of the Bible. Although they may have tried to do good before they knew God, now it becomes a natural thing for them to love other people. Their desires start to change, and they start to willingly give up broken patterns and actions so that God can heal them. The anxiety, depression, and selfishness that was in their life before they knew God starts to become faith, hope, and love. When people look at them, they start to say, "There's something different about you." They start to become an authentic example of Jesus wherever they go and in whatever they do.

You might say, "This is great. I want to live this kind of authentic life, but how does it happen?" Well, before we look at the practical ways it starts to happen in our life, we first have to understand why it can happen.

HOLY SPIRIT

When we surrender to God's grace and start a relationship with God, something amazing happens immediately. The Bible says that in the same instant we receive Jesus and submit to Him as Lord, we receive the Holy Spirit. Thus far in our journey of knowing God, we have discovered there is God the Father and Jesus, who is God the Son. But we haven't yet talked about the third person of what is called the Trinity: God the Holy Spirit. I won't go into great detail about the Trinity, but at its core it is an understanding that God is one God in three persons. So whether we say God the Father, God the Son, or God the Holy Spirit, we are talking about the same God, but speaking about the specific aspects of that person of the Godhead. In surrendering to God's grace, we are not only surrendering to God the Father's mercy, or God the Son's sacrifice, but also to the God the Holy Spirit's presence. Throughout the Bible, we see the power that the Holy Spirit brings about when His presence is there. In the Old Testament, the Holy Spirit is depicted as hovering over the chaotic waters of creation.[19] Now, the Holy Spirit comes upon people to bring wisdom and strength. Before the death and resurrection of Jesus, however, the Holy Spirit only came upon people for a time. After Jesus ascended into heaven, Jesus told the disciples to wait in Jerusalem together until the Holy Spirit came. In Acts 2, Pentecost happens, where the Holy Spirit came to dwell in the disciples. They were empowered to do amazing things. We see Holy Spirit empowered people speak in languages that they don't know, heal people from diseases, and speak boldly in the face of great opposition. Today, the Holy Spirit comes to dwell in every person that surrenders to God's grace.

When I talk about living authentically like Jesus, I am not telling you this kind of living happens simply because you pull up your boot straps and decide to do it. That is the way we think *before* we accept God's grace. Remember, we cannot do anything unless God empowers us to do it. We can live authentically only because the Holy Spirit is reviving us. Revival is a word you may associate with old-time traveling preachers holding weeklong meetings at a church. The hope of those preachers was that the Holy Spirit would work through that week to bring about new life in people. Revival in our lives means that God the Holy Spirit is bringing to life the parts in us that were dead.

Within the past several years, I have taken up the hobby of gardening. My sister-in-law, an agricultural missionary in

Africa, helped me start a small garden. Now, I had never grown anything in my life and wasn't sure if I would be good at it. I learned as much as I could from her and then thoroughly studied some other resources. The garden started out fairly simple, but once I realized how much fun it was to produce my own food, I started to expand what I was doing. Last year I decided to have our biggest garden yet, but it became bigger than I even imagined it would be because of a bad habit I have. You see, toward the end of planting season, local farms sell starter plants really inexpensively. The plants look terrible because they have outgrown their tiny starter pots and most are starting to die. Unfortunately, I am so tempted to buy these plants both because they are super cheap and because I am convinced that I can bring them back to life. What is amazing to me about these almost dead plants is that if you take them home, plant them in some really good soil, give them some fertilizer, water them really well, and protect them from pests, most of them end up thriving and producing great amounts of fruit.

The Holy Spirit does a similar thing within us as he helps us look like Jesus. His role is described in different ways in the New Testament. He is described as empowering us to conquer sin (Romans 8). He is described as producing good attitudes and motivations in us (Galatians 5). He is described as a comforter in times of struggle and the One who produces unity (Philippians 2:1). He is described as empowering us with special gifts that are to be used to bless others (Romans 12; 1 Corinthians 12-14). He brings about the transformation that God the Father wants to do in our lives by reviving us to live like Jesus.

HOW DO I BECOME REVIVED FOR AUTHENTIC LIVING?

We can understand what the goal of authentic living means, and also know why the Holy Spirit is the only reason it can happen within us while still not understanding how it happens in our lives on an everyday basis. There are several ways that we can be revived for authentic living:

1. Practice Spiritual Disciplines.

One of the things I hope you have discovered through this chapter is that we cannot make ourselves live more like Jesus in our own strength. Only the Holy Spirit can do that. So if we want to be revived for authentic living, the goal is less about following rules and more about putting ourselves in a position to be changed. Just like a potter reshapes his clay to make a masterpiece, so our God wants to reshape our life into something beautiful. We just need to be willing to be shaped.

I am the Pastor of Spiritual Formation at my church. I am called that because I oversee most of the groups, classes, and opportunities that would point people towards becoming more like Jesus. We have a definition that we use when we are teaching people what spiritual formation is. It goes like this:

Spiritual formation is the process
by which all of a person (heart, soul, mind, and strength)
is transformed into all of Christ
by the power of the Holy Spirit
through consistent and intentional openness to God
in the practice of spiritual disciplines.

It is a wordy definition, but it summarizes much of what we talked about in this chapter. One of the most important parts of the definition to me is the last section that talks about "consistent and intentional openness to God." Like I said, our job is not to do all of the work ourselves. Our job is to consistently (meaning every day) and intentionally (meaning with purpose) open our lives to God.

Practically, we do this by practicing spiritual disciplines. Richard Foster says in his book *Celebration of Disciplines*, "God has given us the Disciplines of the spiritual life as a means of receiving His grace. The Disciplines allow us to place ourselves before God so that He can transform us...They are God's means of grace."[20] Dallas Willard in his *The Spirit of the Disciplines* says, "A discipline is any activity within our power that we engage in to enable us to do what we cannot do by direct effort."[21] Basically, a spiritual discipline is an intentional action to submit our lives to God that, when done over time, will allow God to change us. These spiritual disciplines include things like reading the Bible, learning to pray, fasting, giving of our tithes and offerings, committing to an intentional accountability relationship with another believer, spending time in solitude and silence in order to listen to God, spending time worshipping God, confessing our sins to someone else, and many other actions. Many of the things I have already encouraged you to do throughout this book have been forms of spiritual discipline. For instance, even back when we talked about being humbled, I encouraged you to start reading the Bible and praying. These practices will leave room for the Holy Spirit to do in us what we cannot do for ourselves.

You might say, "That sounds good, but discipline sounds like a terrible word. How do I keep getting excited about doing something that seems so repetitive and boring?"

Growing up, there is one thing in particular that comes to mind when I think about the word discipline. When I was in elementary school we lived in a parsonage that was owned by the church. There was one room right as you came in the entrance that we called our living room. I am told back then it was common practice to have a living room that was meant to be a place to greet people that came over to visit but was not really used in an everyday fashion. All I know is our living room was decorated beautifully with nice furniture and white carpet, and I was instructed by my mom not to play with my toys in there. The only time I was really allowed to be in there was when I had to practice piano. I started piano lessons when I was young because my sister was taking lessons and I liked music. What I didn't understand is that if my family were going to invest money for me to go to a good teacher, it meant I was expected to practice a significant amount of time each week. On most days I would be asked to practice about forty-five minutes. I would probably try to cheat the system and not practice as much as I should, so my parents put a kitchen timer on the piano. Every time I started practicing, I was supposed to turn that dial to forty-five minutes and not stop practicing until the timer went off. Some days it went by pretty fast. Most days it felt like torture. I would feel like I had practiced for half the time, only to look down and find out the dial had gone down a mere five minutes.

However, you know what was interesting about this discipline of practicing? The more I consistently and intentionally practiced the less boring it became, the more I was excited to get better at particular pieces, and the more opportunities I had to play piano in public. Although in the moment I might have seen discipline as boring and difficult, the longer I practiced that discipline the more thankful to my parents I became for encouraging me to be disciplined. It is not an exact comparison to our practice of spiritual disciplines, but it is pretty close. Spiritual disciplines may seem difficult and uncomfortable at first. You may not feel like they are changing anything when you start them, but if you consistently and intentionally pursue God through spiritual disciplines you will look back and be amazed at what He has done to transform you.

2. Step out in the power of the Holy Spirit.

Disciplines are an important way to learn more about God and to put ourselves in a position to be changed by Him. Another important step in the process of being revived for authentic living is to take a step of faith in the power of the Holy Spirit when He calls us. Recently, I was playing with my son, Judah, at a farm that had activities for young kids. He was up on top of some hay bales and it was arranged so the kids could jump from one bale to the next. I was standing next to Judah and I encouraged him to jump to the next hay bale. You would have thought I had asked him to jump off a tower because he was terrified of jumping the short distance between the two. I tried to help him across and encouraged him to do it, but he just went limp and would not try it. I was disappointed only because I knew the fun he would have if he jumped and from my perspective I knew that he was capable of doing it with my help. Unfortunately, from his perspective all he saw was how big the challenge was and he didn't trust me to help him through it at the time.

I find this is the way our spiritual lives often work as well. God will be leading us, blessing us, transforming us, and we are really excited about it until he leads us to a place that makes us feel uncomfortable. We become uncomfortable because we either don't want to give something up that God is calling us to give up or we don't think we have the ability to do something that God has called us to do. In that moment, we often wither and sit down where we are like Judah did on the hay bale. Even though we know God called us to be obedient in something or take a step of faith in something, we will care more about our own safety and comfort than whether we are being obedient to God. I call this giving God our "no." And there is terrible power in saying "no" to what is right for us to do. I have watched in my own life and in others' lives that until we are willing to change that "no" into a "yes" we will be completely stuck in the place we were at when we gave God our "no." God is a gentleman and He will not force us to change. He waits for us to be obedient and He is very patient in lovingly bringing us around to the place we need to be. But until we are willing to be obedient, we will be completely stuck in the same relational problems, sinful patterns, and wrong thinking we were in when we gave God our "no." It is part of the reason that we see such dismay and apathy among people who would call themselves Christians and are supposed to have the power of Jesus at work in them. Even though they have been raised from death to life, been given salvation, and been given the ability to be transformed by the Holy Spirit, their "no" is blocking them from the fruitful life that they should be living. If we want to truly be revived for authentic living, then we need to stop saying "no" and we have to be willing to step out in the power of the Holy Spirit.

Romans 8 compares and contrasts this life of "no" with a life of "yes." The beginning of Romans 8 begins with the Apostle Paul talking about how there is now no condemnation for those who have surrendered to God's grace. In verses 5-8 he contrasts the lives of two different kinds of people: those who live according to the flesh and those who live according to the Spirit. Those who live according to the Spirit are those who have surrendered to God's grace and those who live according to the flesh are those who still have not accepted Jesus' death and resurrection. Paul says those who live according to the flesh have their minds set on what their flesh desires, the results of their decisions produce death, and they are ultimately hostile to God. They have chosen not to be humbled, broken, or surrendered to God's grace. In contrast, those who live according to the Spirit have their minds set on what the Spirit desires; the results of their life produce life and peace, and their lives are open to the work of God. After Paul summarizes these two lives, he says in Romans 8:9-13,

> *You, however, are not in the realm of the flesh but are in the realm of the Spirit, if indeed the Spirit of God lives in you. And if anyone does not have the Spirit of Christ, they do not belong to Christ. But if Christ is in you, then even though your body is subject to death because of sin, the Spirit gives life because of righteousness. And if the Spirit of him who raised Jesus from the dead is living in you, he who raised Christ from the dead will also give life to your mortal bodies because of his Spirit who lives in you. Therefore, brothers and sisters, we have an obligation—but it is not to the flesh, to live according to it. For if you live according to the flesh, you will die; but if by the Spirit you put to death the misdeeds of the body, you will live.*

Notice what he says about those who have "the Spirit of Him who raised Jesus from the dead" living in them. He says that life will be produced in them "because of His Spirit who lives in you." This is the promise that we have talked about in this chapter: God, the Holy Spirit, can and will revive us to live authentically like Jesus. But there is an obligation that Paul writes about as well. He says our obligation is not to the flesh. If we live according to the flesh, that same death we had in our lives before will be produced in us. Living according to the flesh is giving God our "no." Every time He calls us to do something or step out into something and we deny Him we are simply saying that we trust ourselves and our way of thinking more than we trust God and His ways. Instead of continuing to be humbled by God's eternal truth, we return to trusting ourselves more than Him. Instead of remembering we need to be broken to have a new heart, we start to be okay with doing things that are against God's holy commands. And if we continue to give God our "no" we will sink down into the same kind of despair and death we had before.

The apostle goes on to say in verse 13, "But if by the spirit you put to death the misdeeds of the body, you will live." What He is saying is if we are willing to obey God when He calls us to do something and give God our "yes," the Holy Spirit will enable us to put to death "the misdeeds of the body." For instance, if prior to surrendering to God's grace you had issues with anger, you might have routinely yelled at your family, held grudges with your coworkers, and always have been on the verge of lashing out at people. Jesus lived a life of love that even when He was on the cross (with a right to be angry with the world) He asked God the Father to forgive them for putting Him on the cross. Jesus also said in Matthew 5:44, "But I tell you, love your enemies and pray for those who persecute you." If you have truly surrendered to God's grace and come to find out God wants you to look like Jesus even in terms of your anger, the Holy Spirit will convict you that you need to do something about it. Now, if you decide when you sense this conviction you would rather keep living in anger because it's comfortable, then you will be giving God your "no." Unfortunately, you will not only be denying obedience to the Holy Spirit, you will miss out on the blessings He wants to give you by dealing with your anger. Instead, if every time you start to become angry about something, you stop to pray and ask the Holy Spirit to take your anger away and give you love for the people that you're angry at, He will start to change and transform who you are. You will start to naturally love people and He will give you more and more opportunities to express this love in the context of situations that used to make you angry. The more often and the more emphatically you are willing to give God your "yes," the faster and more completely He will transform you.

Here's the thing, however. Part of the reason we are more likely to give God our "no" and to stay where we are at instead of continuing to be transformed by Him is that it is easier to just pretend to have the name "Christian" instead of living like Christ. Some of us have this misguided notion that the minute we surrender to God's grace, everything in our life will become easy and comfortable. Living life with Jesus is wonderful, amazing, and glorious, but it is not always easy. We were designed to know God and worship God, but until we have left this earth and are in His presence for eternity, there will always be a battle being waged in us and around us. We must understand this in order to pursue the life God wants for us. We must understand God has given us the power to live like Jesus, but if we continually give God our "no" because we are uncomfortable we will squander the power God has given us. One of the saddest things in the entire world to me is to watch people who claim to follow Jesus continually live lives that do not look anything like Jesus because they are unaware of the power they have in Christ. It reminds me of the electrical system of a building. We had to do some work to the electrical system of the home we purchased last year and during installation there was a time when the power was out. Even if we wanted to be able to turn the lights on or turn the furnace on there was nothing we could do. There was no power running to the house. But imagine that after we had the system replaced we would walk into the house excited about seeing the new work that was done and then being disappointed because there were no lights on. But none of us would do that, because anyone who has lived in a house understands that even if there is power running to the house, a person must still take the action of turning on the light switch.

In a similar way, before we come to know God, there is nothing we can do to honor God or conquer sin. There is no "power" in our lives. After surrendering to God's grace, the "power" of the Holy Spirit is now present in our lives and this isn't just any power. This is the same power, according to the Apostle Paul, that raised Jesus from the dead. This is supernatural, unending power capable of changing any circumstance and conquering any sin. But unless we are willing to ask God to lead us and guide us every day and then to give God our "yes" when He calls us to take a step of faith, we still will not have any of those "light switches" turned on. That is the thing about faith – God often desires us to take the step of faith to trust Him before He releases His power to accomplish what He has called us to do.

Where is God calling you to take a step of faith right now? This question is not only for those who are just beginning their journey of faith, but also for anyone who is at any stage of their spiritual journey. The process of being revived for authentic living starts the moment we surrender to God's grace and never ends until we are in the presence of

God for eternity. Some people think after a long time of knowing God they have gotten everything in order and are just going to coast the rest of the way until they get to heaven. This is not the way of Jesus. Each one of us who has truly surrendered to God's grace knows that as we continue to humble ourselves before God there are still broken parts of us that need to be revived. We all are being called to look more like Jesus everyday. In the final chapters we will look at the two primary areas where this revival process happens in our lives, but unless we are able to understand this step of revival in the process of knowing God, the other two will not make sense. Before you continue, I encourage you to take some time to reflect and ask the Lord if you are saying "no" to Him in any area of your life.

REFLECTION QUESTIONS

1. We talked about how there are different ways of using the word "know." There are various levels of knowing something or someone. You could know about someone, you could know someone's like and dislikes, you could know someone's deepest thoughts and dreams, etc. If we put "knowing" in those terms, how well do you think you know God?

2. The basic point of authentic living is God's grace transforming our everyday life. It is the process of God making us look more like Jesus in how we talk, act, think, and feel. In which areas of your life do you sense the most resistance to letting God transform you? Why?

3. We talked about the virtual reality goggles and our reaction to letting God transform us. Out of the different reactions we could have, which one did you identify with the most?

Why?

4. The Holy Spirit seems to be very misunderstood by most people. Why do you think this is and what did you learn from this chapter about the role of the Holy Spirit in our lives?

5. Spiritual disciplines are an essential part of us knowing God. Do you find it difficult to practice spiritual disciplines on a regular basis? If so, why?

6. We talked about the power of "no" and the power of "yes" in this chapter. If we say "no" to God, we will be stuck in the same spot until we are willing to say "yes" to what He called us to do. Is there something in your life you have said "no" to God about?

7. Which of the application steps below will be most difficult for you? Why?

APPLICATION

1. Spiritual Disciplines – Pick one new spiritual discipline to start practicing on a regular basis. Disciplines encompass many things including reading the bible, fasting, worship, silence, prayer, journaling, or other spiritual disciplines. If you need help learning how to practice these disciplines, find someone who has experience in practicing these disciplines and follow their lead. Or look for resources like *Celebration of Disciplines* by Richard Foster.

2. Take a Step of Faith – Pick one area of your life where you know you are living in your own strength instead of trusting God to do something more (examples: your money, time, energy, relationships, etc). Take a step of faith and say "yes" to surrendering that area of your life to Jesus.

Step 5
THANKFUL FOR GROWING RELATIONSHIPS

After being revived for authentic living and beginning to look like Christ, there are two more steps of knowing God that might sound unusual. The first of these steps we will call being "thankful for growing relationships." You might wonder why growing relationships would be part of the process of knowing God? First, knowing God is about having a relationship with God, not just a religion to follow. If we desire to know God to the fullest extent, we must be growing in this relationship. Second, in the Bible God tells us that loving other people and growing in relationship with others is a sign that we know Him and are growing in our relationship with Him. In the book of 1 John it talks about God and His love for us. At one point in 1 John 4:19-21, it says, "We love because he first loved us. Whoever claims to love God yet hates a brother or sister is a

91

liar. For whoever does not love their brother and sister, whom they have seen, cannot love God, whom they have not seen. And he has given us this command: Anyone who loves God must also love their brother and sister." There are a lot of so-called Christians out there who would claim to have a relationship with God, but consistently treat the people around them terribly. They are hateful, rude, ignorant, and unloving. John would call these people liars. People who love God should also love others around them. Growing relationships are an integral part of knowing God.

You might also wonder why the ENGAGE step we have for growing relationships is "to be thankful." In a world where we are always expected to take grandiose actions and we put a lot of pressure on ourselves to perform, simply being thankful seems weak. How hard is it to be thankful? But take one look at the world and you realize that thankfulness as an attitude is dying out. As it dies out, people increasingly have no desire for sincerely growing relationships. They are satisfied to simply coexist with the people around them and tolerate people. But God has called us to truly satisfying and refreshing relationships. So why aren't we thankful for these growing relationships, if that is how they are supposed to be? Growing relationships take hard work, self-denial, and all of the things we have talked about thus far: humility, brokenness, surrender, and revival. Many times, instead of being a little uncomfortable in order to keep growing (like we talked about last chapter), we decide to settle for comfort. And comfort puts our attention back on us where it shouldn't be if we are trying to know God.

I think that is why God calls us to be thankful so often in the Bible. Thankfulness is an immediate and simple action we can take to turn our attention to God and to the blessings we have in relationships. Here are some examples of passages that mention thankfulness in the Bible:

"Let the peace of Christ rule in your hearts, since as members of one body you were called to peace. And be **thankful**." – Colossians 3:15

"Devote yourselves to prayer, being watchful and **thankful**." – Colossians 4:2

"Therefore, since we are receiving a kingdom that cannot be shaken, let us be **thankful**, and so worship God acceptably with reverence and awe." – Hebrews 12:28

"...rooted and built up in him, strengthened in the faith as you were taught, and overflowing with **thankfulness**." – Colossians 2:7

"This service that you perform is not only supplying the needs of the Lord's people but is also overflowing in many expressions of **thanks** to God." – 2 Corinthians 9:12

"**Thanks** be to God for his indescribable gift!" – 2 Corinthians 9:15

"I have not stopped giving **thanks** for you, remembering you in my prayers." – Ephesians 1:16

"...always giving **thanks** to God the Father for everything, in the name of our Lord Jesus Christ." – Ephesians 5:20

"I **thank** my God every time I remember you." – Philippians 1:3

"We always **thank** God, the Father of our Lord Jesus Christ, when we pray for you." – Colossians 1:3

"...and giving joyful **thanks** to the Father, who has qualified you to share in the inheritance of his holy people in the kingdom of light." – Colossians 1:12

"How can we **thank** God enough for you in return for all the joy we have in the presence of our God because of you?" – 1 Thessalonians 3:9

We are called to be thankful for God, for His blessings, for other people, and for the blessings we get from relationship with them. First, we will look at what it means to have growing relationships and second, we will figure out exactly what it looks like to engage in thankfulness on a daily basis.

WHAT RELATIONSHIPS?

There are billions of people on this planet. How are we supposed to know what relationships to invest in? God encourages us in the Bible to have a responsibility to all people in the world to some extent, but there is definitely a hierarchy of relationship. Understanding this hierarchy is essential to us knowing how to invest our energies in helping those relationships grow. Do you remember when you had yearbooks in junior high and high school? You would always be hunting down your best friends to get them to sign your yearbook and they would be doing the same. If you were to look back at those yearbooks, you would see a lot of messages that say, "I won't ever forget you and we won't ever lose touch after school." However, how many people do you still have contact with from your high school days? One? Two? Maybe even none? The reason it is so hard to keep in contact is you might go off to college and meet more people, then find someone and get married, then meet new people in the workplace, then have kids, etc. At some point, it is impossible to invest in relationships with everyone you meet.

So how do we make sure we keep our relationships in the right order? In Luke 10:25 it says, "On one occasion an expert in the law stood up to test Jesus. 'Teacher,' he asked, 'what must I do to inherit eternal life?'" He responds in Luke 10:27 by affirming this order of relationships: "'Love the Lord your God with all your heart and with all your soul and with all your strength and with all your mind'; and, 'Love your neighbor as yourself.'" The first differentiation we see is we are clearly supposed to love God first and foremost. And not just love Him. We are supposed to love Him with everything that we are: our heart, soul, strength, and mind. This is everything that defines us, everything that we do, and everything we use to accomplish those things. He is to be our highest motivation, the reason behind every thought we have, and our greatest joy. This love is supposed to outweigh any other love we have by a long shot. In fact, Jesus said in Matthew 10:37, "Anyone who loves their father or mother more than me is not worthy of me; anyone who loves their son or daughter more than me is not worthy of me." He is not telling us that we shouldn't love our family, but He is making the point that our love for God should far outweigh any love we have for any other person, no matter who it is.

OUR RELATIONSHIP WITH GOD

You might say, "I understand that I need to love God,

but saying that I need to love God with everything that defines me and love Him far more than anyone else around me sounds a little intense and harsh. How am I ever supposed to live a life like that especially when I feel like my relationship with Him is so weak at this point?" I understand how you feel, especially when most of us have never seen proper godly relationships throughout our lives. I do prayer counseling with people on a regular basis and one of the most common things I hear about is the dysfunctional relationships people have had in their lives. Whether it is dysfunctional parents, spouses, churches, or friends, I have found that most people have not seen a godly picture of what relationship or community is supposed to be. And like we discussed last chapter about the virtual reality glasses, if that is the only type of relationship we have ever seen, we will have a hard time understanding that God wants something completely different in our lives. This is why Jesus calls us to a growing relationship with Him before calling us to love anyone else. If we are to ever love other people in a godly way, we have to first let God love us and show us how to love.

When I was on summer break between my junior and senior years of college, I had a really interesting example of why it is so important to keep growing in our relationship with God first and foremost above all other things. My life was a little out of balance in college. For most of my college career I was juggling three or four majors, working in ministry positions on campus, travelling with music groups I was involved in, and trying to participate in social events. In my head, I rationalized how all of these things were so important because I was trying to serve God in all of them. I was being trained in my education to be a pastor, I was ministering to students on campus, I was leading worship music for people, and I was trying to build godly friendships. One of the unfortunate side effects of this pattern of living is that my relationship with God stopped growing. I would still try to spend time with God, but I had so many things crowding my schedule that He was becoming an "add-on" to my life of ministry. I soon found out that the results of this way of living were catching up to me. Normally, I spent summers with my parents and when I started college they moved to a different state than where I grew up. That meant when I stayed there for the summer I did not know many people except some family that was in the area. I would simply get a summer job, spend some time with family, and then relax.

The summer after my junior year was different. I was so burned out from my overcrowded life. One day, I was working on a computer at my job and an overwhelming feeling of dread came into me. My heart began racing and my palms were sweaty. I had no idea what was going on. After things calmed down, I realized I must have been having a panic attack. That wasn't all though. In general, I was apathetic. I didn't feel much of anything, and yet there was restlessness in my spirit. I had never been on depression medicine before and did not know how I felt about it, but I figured I should go to the doctor and get checked out. I told the doctor the things that were happening and without giving me any other advice or suggestions he just wrote me a prescription for anti-depressants. I do not deny there are some people who need depression medication for imbalances or other issues, but I had a sneaking suspicion this had more to do with a soul imbalance than a physical imbalance in my case. I simply started to practice what this book talks about in my relationship with God. It had been so long since I had really intentionally invested in my relationship with God and spent quality time with Him. As I sought God out, He was faithful to speak to me. I was bringing all of the pain and garbage that was going on in my soul to Him and one day as I read Zephaniah 3:17 I felt as though God were speaking it over me. He said, "The Lord your God is with you, He is mighty to save. He will take great delight in you, He will quiet you with His love, He will rejoice over you with singing." In the context of the Old Testament book of Zephaniah this was spoken to the Israelite people, but in the context of my life at the time I sensed God saying through it, "Don't forget you cannot do all of this on your own! I am the One who saved you, I am the One who will continue to use you to bless others, and I am the One who empowers you. Without my love, you cannot be filled up to love others." I pictured Him as the loving Father He is, taking delight in me as His child, quieting me with His love like a father quiets his distraught child, and singing a song of joy over me. I was so broken at that time, realizing more than anything else my hierarchy of relationships had gotten out of balance. I had assumed that with a "little dose of Jesus" I could live this busy life pouring into all kinds of people and things. Unless our first and greatest aim is the love of God, we will never experience love and be able to pass that love on to others. When I started to have a growing relationship with Jesus again, I found complete freedom from the panic attacks and depression I was experiencing.

Again, I understand there are people who may need medication for their particular case, but this example has less to do with the depression and more to do with the fact that when we stop having a growing relationship with Jesus everything else in our life goes awry. This is why Jesus directs us to love God with everything we are and to put our relationship with Him above anything else.

OUR RELATIONSHIPS WITH OUR FAMILY

After we have prioritized having a growing relationship with God, the next level of relationships in our life according to Scripture is our family. Essential to understanding what growing relationships mean for families is understanding what God's intention was for family, how His love is to be expressed within families, and how godly family relationships are used to impact the world.

Families began as far back as the first two chapters of the book of Genesis. In the act of creating everything, God created Adam and gave him the task of naming the other animals. In Genesis 2:20-24 it says:

So the man gave names to all the livestock, the birds in the sky and all the wild animals. But for Adam no suitable helper was found. So the LORD God caused the man to fall into a deep sleep; and while he was sleeping, he took one of the man's ribs and then closed up the place with flesh. Then the LORD God made a woman from the rib he had taken out of the man, and he brought her to the man. The man said, "This is now bone of my bones and flesh of my flesh; she shall be called 'woman,' for she was taken out of man." That is why a man leaves his father and mother and is united to his wife, and they become one flesh.

It is interesting to think that Adam needed someone else in his world since he already had a clear and uncompromised relationship with God. You would assume his relationship with God would fulfill him completely, yet remember how we were created in the image of God. God is one God in three persons. Even in the Trinity, there is community. And if we are created in His image, then there would be a need inside of

99

us to give love to someone on our same level. As Kidner says, "The naming of the animals, a scene which portrays man as monarch of all he surveys, poignantly reveals him as a social being, made for fellowship, not power: he will not live until he loves, giving himself away to another on his own level."[22] We were made to be social creatures and the foundational element of our social life from the beginning was the family. As you can see, verse 24 gives this passage and our need for fellowship as the reason why families exist. Now, not all of us are married, but whether we are married or single we all have families of some kind. We all have the family into which we were born or adopted. The purpose of these family relationships was to be a place for fellowship and love.

However, even if that is the purpose, it doesn't answer how God expected that fellowship to be found within the family. There is so much said about the family in the Bible and there is no way we could possibly cover it all in this chapter. If we were to summarize God's commands on family relationships, though, I believe we could conclude that God intends for families to be a place where God's love is expressed in an experiential way. Families are to be the laboratories of God's grace, a place where through trial and error the love of God is worked out in tangible ways. In order to function in this way, each member of a family is supposed to live out God's love in a particular way. Ephesians 5 summarizes some of these expectations for each member of the family. Before any of the commands are given, there is a summary statement in Ephesians 5:21 that can be applied to any family relationship, "Submit to one another out of reverence of Christ." The overarching attitude that should be present in any growing family relationship and truthfully, any relationship in general, is an attitude of submission.

The word "submit" does not make sense to many people. It is such a negative word to those who have been in abusive relationships or who believe strongly in their own rights and independence above all else. They might say, "Why should I submit to anyone especially when they might not treat me as well as I believe I should be treated?" Well, first, I want to make sure nobody thinks being in a place of continual abuse is appropriate. I have talked to many people who live in abusive marriages and abusive homes. If someone in your home is physically or sexually abusing you it is so imperative to reach out for help and figure out the steps required to take yourself out of that situation for a time so both you and the person abusing you can receive God's grace.

Even if you are not in a situation of active abuse, the word "submit" might still sound so strange because it is in direct conflict to the entire mindset of our society. Our entire world has flipped upside down in terms of what God desires for relationships and in a very deceptive way. We talk constantly about our rights, while at the same time refusing to submit to the One who gives us any rights. We wonder why husbands and fathers don't live up to the expectations women have for them while at the same time women are told they shouldn't submit to their husbands in any way because they are powerful and don't need a husband. We wonder why wives are constantly insecure and why husbands do not show proper love to their wives when our society keeps pushing the boundaries of sexualizing everything. We wonder why fathers are constantly failing at their role while at the same time portraying most men and fathers as idiots in every sitcom. We wonder why mothers are constantly struggling to live up to expectations while at the same time telling them that women are supposed to fulfill every role in the entire family at the same time. We wonder why our kids turn out wrong since we provide them with a completely "safe" life and every activity and technology known to man while realizing that "safe" lives and constant activity do not provide what kids are really yearning for. We wonder why families keep breaking down while at the same time we refuse to listen to God about how He has designed the family and refuse to submit to one another out of love for Christ. The foundational element behind this destruction of the family is selfishness, the very root of sin itself. We care more about our own path than God's path, we care more about our own needs than the needs of others, and we do not trust anyone else except ourselves. In this world of constant liabilities, we want to measure out our love and make sure there is always some love left over for us. We are taught that loving our family starts with loving ourselves and don't even consider the fact we can't really love anyone (including ourselves) if we don't receive God's love.

God's way stands in direct contrast to the world's perspective and this should make us happy because obviously the world's way of doing family is not working. Ephesians 5 starts with speaking to husbands and wives. It says that wives should submit to their husbands and husbands should love their wives, and it uses the example of Jesus and the church to give the basis for why they should live like this. These are lofty expectations. In the same way that Jesus gave up everything for us, even His life, husbands are supposed to love their wives to such a great extent that they are willing on a daily basis to sacrifice everything. They are to love their wives to the extent that they are willing to sacrifice their own preferences, desires, time, money, and energy in order to show them this love. A husband is to love his wife to the extent that he is willing to give up his life for her. Wives are to submit to their husbands like the church does to Jesus, meaning they should be willing to do the same things husbands are called to do but in a slightly different way. They are to give their husbands love and respect by being willing to listen, willing to follow, and willing to sacrifice their time and energy. This is how a growing relationship is to be between a husband and wife.

You might say, "How could I ever live a life like this? I mean, what about my desires? How will I ever make sure I get what I need and desire if I am giving all of this love to my spouse knowing they might not do the same thing back?" I said earlier that family breakdown comes from selfishness. The only way we can break this cycle of selfishness and have a growing relationship with our spouse is to receive the healing love of God and recognize marriage is not for getting but giving. Think about the example of Jesus and the church. Jesus did not come to earth to get something from us. He came to give something to us. We do not respond to Jesus' love solely to get something from Him (even though we receive everything from Him), but to give ourselves completely to Him because He is worthy of our lives. The primary reason for being in relationship is to give, not to receive. For most of us, we grew up thinking that getting married was in order to get something. Even though we receive many things from marriage, the primary reason God has for marriage is to be a laboratory testing ground to teach us to love and give of ourselves more than we ever thought possible.

My wife and I read a book by Gary Thomas before we got married called *Sacred Marriage*. In it, he makes a powerful case for marriage being more about making us holy than making us happy. It helped me gain a perspective that in every aspect of my marriage relationship (time, finances, sexual intimacy, etc.) the question for me to ask is not, "Am I getting enough from this right now?" The question I should be asking is, "Am I giving of myself to the extent that God has called me to give to my wife right now?" The standard is pretty high for me as a husband. I am supposed to love to the extent of even giving up my own life. The interesting thing I have found is when I am willing to follow God's way and care about my wife and her needs over my own, I experience the love of God more than I would by trying to focus on what I want. The words of Jesus are quoted in Acts 20:35, "It is more blessed to give than to receive." I have found it to be so true in terms of the relationship with my wife.

Growing relationships look similar in terms of parent and child relationships. I remember the first weeks after our son, Judah, was born. I had previously come to terms with how God uses marriage to make us holy and was willing to be unselfish to the extent it took to love my wife. But parenting has a way of stretching you to a point of revealing selfishness you did not even know you had. Many people like the idea of having a baby in their life, but when they realize this little child will be completely dependent on them for everything it becomes overwhelming. Children take more time, money, and energy than any other relationship you could have.

I think this is one of the reasons that our society's attitude toward children has changed dramatically in the past decades. The Bible says in the Psalm 127:3, "Children are a gift from the Lord; they are a reward from him."[23] This is how children were viewed throughout most of world history. They were a gift and reward. Children were desired. In our post-Christian day and age, however, the attitude toward children has become increasingly hostile. There are still many parents that desire children and feel like they are a blessing, but it is more common in our day and age to see people care more about convenience, comfort, and control than children. Millions of babies have died through abortion in recent history simply because having a child was not thought to be "convenient." Millions of other children have been born, but are born to irresponsible parents who get mad with their children simply because they "cramp their lifestyle." And countless other parents have children, but spend more time complaining about their children than caring for them. My wife would read what I call "mommy blogs" after our son was born and there were some really good ones. But I warned her to be careful about which ones she read because there were many other blogs that would simply air grievances about being a mother instead of encouraging godly motherhood. In their attempt to be "authentic" they were giving themselves a right to complain. Complaining is the complete opposite attitude of thankfulness that we are talking about in this chapter. Opening the door to complaining allows self-centeredness to take root, which if not dealt with, leads to apathetic relationships with God and others.

The point is this: A society's treatment of the least of these (children, elderly, and those with special needs) demonstrates the extent of God's working in it. Our society, unsurprisingly, demonstrates a callous and selfish attitude toward children. We must not buy into this mindset if we are to follow Jesus. If we have experienced His grace, we are to treat our role with our children as stewards. In Ephesians 5, it encourages children to honor their parents and then it says, "Fathers, do not exasperate your children; instead, bring them up in the training and instruction of the Lord." This is a demonstration of the spirit of Christian parenting which is to be stewardship. We are to treat our children as a gift from God and see our role as the stewards of a gift He has given us. This will affect our attitude toward our children and also how we raise them.

Our son was two weeks past his due date when he was born. My wife was attempting to have a natural birth and she started into prodromal labor, which is early labor that lasts for a long time and does not progress. She was in this early labor for days, and finally ended up in the hospital for a C-section. In the midst of the C-section some complications arose. In their attempt to get our son's lung to function properly, they intubated him and he developed a tension pneumothorax (a hole in his lung that was filling with air). All I saw from the recovery room was my lifeless son being rushed down the hallway surrounded by medical personnel. The doctors seemed pretty grim over those first couple hours about our son's situation. If they didn't stop the hole in his lung, there was a chance he could die. Finally, we got the news that they were able to stabilize Judah. We were so grateful and thankful. Each day Judah gained strength and he left the NICU one week later, a healthy baby boy. The whole situation helped us treat our son as he was supposed to be treated, as a gift from God. Any time there has been a temptation in our hearts toward convenience, comfort, or complaining in raising him, his birth has been another reminder to us of our role as stewards. Growing relationships between parents and children should be one of obedience and stewardship.

Families were created to fill our need for fellowship. They are to be laboratories of God's grace, where we are to "submit to one another out of reverence for Christ." Husbands and wives are to love each other like Christ and the church. Parents are meant to be stewards of their children, recognizing that they are a gift from God. And God's purpose is for this dynamic, growing family to be a multiplying force on the planet for His Kingdom. In the book of Genesis, God's command to Adam and Eve and then to Noah and his family was to be fruitful and multiply. This was in direct reference to having children, but I think the same notion can be applied to the Christian family. Jesus called us as the church to multiply disciples in the world around us. We will talk more about this in the next chapter, but the family is the first and most intense framework for this multiplication. A growing and thriving Christian family can pass on faith generationally, but also can be a shining light of God's grace in the midst of their everyday interactions. As I said earlier, there are so many people in this world who have never seen the kind of relationships that God intends for us. Many people have never seen a loving and unselfish father, a peace-filled and respectful mother, and obedient children who are content. The light of a godly, growing family can be a beacon of hope for so many people. I believe God intends for families to take on this charge and then open the door of their home to others so they can understand the love of God in a tangible way. I am not saying our families will ever be perfect. Instead, I am saying if we are thankful for growing relationships in our lives because of Jesus, our families could be used to multiply the love of God in the world.

OUR RELATIONSHIPS WITHIN THE BODY OF CHRIST

The Bible teaches us we are also to have growing relationships with those within the church or the body of Christ. Throughout the New Testament, the church is referred to as the body of Christ because it is a picture of the interconnected relationships that should exist between Christians. Much of the New Testament is written to churches of that day and age about how to live out faith together. All of us recognize that living in relationship with other people can be difficult. Gossip, selfish attitudes, anger, coveting, and many other negative things are commonplace in relationships. Many people have even experienced this type of environment at churches they have attended. This is not God's intention. The church, like the family, should be a representation of the kind of relationships that God desires. In John 13:34-35 Jesus says, "A new commandment I give you: Love one another. As I have loved you, so also you must love one another. By this all men will know that you are my disciples if you love one another." Jesus' vision of His church was to be a place where love so permeated everything that it would be evident they were His followers.

These types of relationships are described more fully in Romans 12. In Romans 12:9-18 it says:

Love must be sincere. Hate what is evil; cling to what is good. Be devoted to one another in love. Honor one another above yourselves. Never be lacking in zeal, but keep your spiritual fervor, serving the Lord. Be joyful in hope, patient in affliction, faithful in prayer. Share with the Lord's people who are in need. Practice hospitality. Bless those who persecute you; bless and do not curse. Rejoice with those who rejoice; mourn with those who mourn. Live in harmony with one another. Do not be proud, but be willing to associate with people of low position. Do not be conceited. Do not repay anyone evil for evil. Be careful to do what is right in the eyes of everyone. If it is possible, as far as it depends on you, live at peace with everyone.

On the initial reading of this passage, it just seems like a list of obligations. The idea that we should be thinking about all of these "obligations" all the time can be overwhelming. I believe we could view this passage less like a list of obligations and more like a list of evidences about what true Christian community should look like. True, growing relationships within the church should have sincere love, devotion to one another, honor, zeal, joy, patience, faithfulness, generosity, hospitality, harmony, humility, forgiveness, and peace. Church is supposed to be a place where the typical structure of relationships is turned upside down.

You will find fake, artificial love outside of the church, but within the church love is to be sincere and true. Friends may leave you in a heartbeat outside of the church, but relationships within the church are to be strong and true through the deepest struggles. Relationships outside the church might tear you down, but inside the church you are to be built up. Outside the church, it is expected that people will respond in kind, hurting those who hurt them, but inside the church love should be the response no matter how we're treated. Outside the church, competition and striving for popularity keep people from associating with others who might hurt their image, but inside the church there are to be no divisions like that. Instead, the most prominent person serves the least of these.

I started a young adult ministry at our church a few years ago. One of the ways I knew God was starting to work in the lives of the people that were attending is because I saw this kind of growing relationship happen within the group. When I looked around at the small groups gathered at the end of the night there would be a successful lawyer, a former drug addict, a person with special needs, a popular college student, a talented musician, and someone else struggling with questions about God all at the same table. They would laugh, encourage one another, confess real struggles in their lives, pray for one another, and talk about connecting with each other throughout the week to make sure they were growing stronger in their faith. It dawned on me: where else in the world could you find this combination of successful and struggling people coming together with no pretense, simply desiring to talk about real things and encourage each other? The church is meant to be a special place demonstrating God's grace.

So what helps the church continue to be this kind of place? You might say, "That's nice for you, but I have never found a church experience like that. Most of the churches I have been associated with are full of the biggest hypocrites I have ever met." The question is valid and I wish I had a fancy answer to give you. However, the answer is really the repetition of all the things said so far in this book. Remember, in the beginning how I told you not to trust every "Christian" and every church you come across? Just because someone claims something doesn't mean they truly represent it. And even if a church is trying to represent God's way of growing relationships, it is not easy. The same things we have talked about including lack of humility, lack of brokenness, lack of surrendering, and lack of revival in peoples' lives can keep a church from being the kind of place it is supposed to be. Similar to what we said about marriage relationships, the real question for all of us who have surrendered to God's grace is not necessarily what we are going to get out of church, but what we are willing to give.

A couple friends of mine from college demonstrated this perfectly. I was really close to this particular group of guys from the dorm I lived in for three years and many of them were hoping to serve in churches after school. We spread out all over the country after college and tried to keep in touch. We all ended up in very different situations. Some of them ended up in thriving churches and others ended up serving in difficult church situations. What I respected about my friends is that even if they ended up in difficult situations they did not complain about it. Instead, they simply tried to be a faithful example of what Jesus would look like in those communities. And, not surprisingly, many of them started to become major forces of change within those communities. If we are thankful for growing relationships, our perspective within a church community will be about serving others instead of complaining that our needs are not being met.

OUR RELATIONSHIPS WITH THE WORLD AROUND US

Finally, the Bible also encourages us over and over again to intentionally have growing relationships with people in the world around us. Now, you might say, "I've got that covered already. I mean, I know people at work, I know people in my neighborhood, and I know people at my gym." While it's true each one of us has a network of relationships within the world, it doesn't mean those relationships are growing relationships. God desires that we would have intentionally growing relationships with those around us so we can show them His love and let them know the Good News about Jesus. We will talk more about this in the next chapter, but I did not want to leave it out of our understanding of the priority of relationships we need to have within our lives.

HOW TO BE THANKFUL FOR GROWING RELATIONSHIPS

Hopefully at this point you understand what "growing relationships" mean and look like within our lives. We are to intentionally invest in our relationships with God, our family, our church, and the world. These are to be relationships that grow in our demonstration of the love of God and teach us how to live like Jesus lived. As they grow, we will find our relationships and our lives become more satisfying, fruitful, and meaningful. You may have read this chapter and been more burdened than relieved. It seems like a large task. Actually, to live this out perfectly is an impossible task for us if we do not know Jesus. Even if we do know Jesus, it can seem like a gargantuan task. Like I said at the beginning of the chapter, I think this overwhelming feeling is why we feel the need to respond in extravagant ways when things are wrong in our relationships. We buy a really expensive gift for our spouse to rekindle a dying marriage, we take our kids on a trip to try to replace all the time we lost with them, we spend hours working on a large project at church in order to make up for poor relationships with other church members, or we hand out tracts to people believing that if we do that every once in a while it will make up for a lack of growing relationships with people that do not know Jesus. Do these grandiose responses really change anything? At best, they change things for a short time, but the underlying rhythm of relationships within our lives will still not look like Jesus.

That is why I believe a simple heart change every day will do more to grow our relationships than any occasionally impressive action could. I believe very strongly that the trajectory of our lives is more important than the current position of our lives. I recently read an article describing retirement resources.[24] It showed how much you would make if you started in your twenties, thirties, forties, and so on. The interesting thing to me is if you start putting away what seems like an insignificant amount of money every year when you are in your twenties, it is possible for you to have over half a million dollars by the time you retire. Someone who is in their twenties might say, "I have so little to give. It's not even worth it." But if they start with what they have and consistently give a little every day, every week, every month, and every year they will find that the trajectory of their retirement will continue to escalate.

The same thing is true of our spiritual lives. If you allow yourself to be humbled, broken, surrendered, and revived more and more every day you will find that although your relationships seem completely out of whack now, the trajectory of those relationships will continue to change. I have talked to many people who want to grow in their faith and want to impact the world for Jesus, but they feel like their lives before Jesus were so sinful and broken, how could God ever use them? I would give them the same encouragement: it's not about your current position. It's about your trajectory. The problem is, even if we desire to keep growing with Jesus in our relationships, relationships are messy. It can be so easy to get sidetracked, to stop depending on God for our strength in relationships, and all of a sudden those relationships in our lives that used be growing become stagnant.

The greatest antidote I have found to becoming stagnant in my relationships is thankfulness. 1 Thessalonians 5:16-18 says, "Rejoice always, pray continually, give thanks in all circumstances; for this is God's will for you in Christ Jesus." Rejoicing, praying, and giving thanks are all ways of keeping our attention on the only One who can help the situation anyway. There are three ways in particular that I believe we need to be thankful.

1. Be thankful for the people God has placed in your life.

Growing relationships stop growing the minute you stop seeing them in their proper light. For those relationships God has placed in your life including those with your church, spouse, children, and others, thankfulness is the antidote to selfishness. Selfishness causes us to jump from one relationship to another looking for someone to make us happy. Thankfulness allows us to remember God might have reasons for a particular relationship beyond just making us happy. What if God's purpose in keeping you at a church with power struggles is for you to be part of the solution of bringing love instead of manipulation? What if God's purpose in a difficult marriage is to teach you to be faithful so your spouse can finally find God's love? What if God's purpose for having you in a difficult workplace is to remind you how you need to depend on Him daily? For most of us, if we are in a difficult place our first reaction is to run. We may even "blame" God by saying He wouldn't want us to be in this kind of difficulty. If you read the Bible, however, you will find that God led His people through many different struggles on purpose. He did this because experiencing difficulty and struggle is the only way to grow. You can't grow muscles at the gym unless the resistance of your exercise starts to break up your muscle tissue and allow it to grow. God has placed you exactly where He wants you for a reason. When we are thankful for those God has placed in our lives, we are telling God we trust Him to provide the love we need to continue to grow in those relationships.

2. Be thankful for relationships and situations that test your own "limits of love."

This goes hand in hand with the previous encouragement and is simply a continuation of it. If we are thankful for the people God has placed in our lives, even if they are difficult, we can be thankful for situations that test our own "limits of love." Imagine that the love we can show on our own without depending on God's strength is like a cup. The cup is only so big and can only be poured out so far. This is our own "limit of love." There are actually Christians who never show love past their own "limit of love." They ration out their love instead of being generous; they make a point to be a "martyr" if they have given more than they think is comfortable, and they spend much of their time and energy on themselves so they can keep their "cups full." I am so heartbroken for these Christians. They have missed out on what God wants to do in their lives. God never wanted us to depend on our own "limit of love." He wants to grow our faith to depend on His "limit of love" which is endless. His love is never ending and complete. His love extends to the worst of sinners and heals the darkest wounds. His love changes situations instead of being changed by the situation. There is no limit to His love.

We discover we are starting to understand the necessity of growing relationships when we begin to be thankful for situations that test our "limits of love." Maybe you are the wife of an unmotivated husband. You are striving every day to care for the kids, the home, and the finances, and all your husband does is go to work and then comes home and watches TV. You might be carrying around so much anger, emptiness, and anxiety because of this situation. Your anger at your husband may have gotten to the point where you can barely even look at him. Here's the thing: conventional wisdom would tell you that you are justified in your anger. Even church people would feel sorry for you and might tell you some not-so-nice things you should say to this husband of yours. The relationship is practically dead and not moving in any good direction. You are far past your limit of love and you are not sure there is anything you can do about it.

It might sound challenging, but I think the greatest faith step you could take is to be thankful for God's relationship with you, thankful for your relationship with your husband, and thankful that God is using this situation to test your own "limits of love." I have seen women in similar situations live this out everyday over a period of time, and even if their husband never changes, their faith, hope, and love continue to grow exponentially. Many times, the husbands do change, however, and come to a point of salvation themselves. We see an encouragement of this in 1 Peter 3:1-2, "Wives, in the same way submit yourselves to your own husbands so that, if any of them do not believe the word, they may be won over without words by the behavior of their wives, when they see the purity and reverence of your lives."

This same test of our "limit of love" can be played out in a thousand different ways with all kinds of situations. Now, (as was said earlier in the chapter) this does not mean there are times when it is important to remove yourself from a person or situation in order for both of you to find healing. If there is a continual pattern of intentional pain coming to you from a person in your life, it very well may be a situation that God would want to remove you from for a time while healing is found. So at the same time we can be thankful for God testing our "limit of love," we must listen to the Lord in order to see whether He wants us to stay put or get out of the situation for a time.

3. Be thankful every day for another opportunity to show God's love.

This last one seems simple but it is so powerful. Maybe we can be thankful for a day, a week, a month, or a year, but there will come a limit to our own ability to be thankful. In that time, it is another test of the "limit of love." The most powerful thing we can do, even when we don't feel thankful, is to ask God to make us thankful. When we can wake up everyday being thankful for another opportunity to show His love, whether we feel like it or not, powerful things start to happen. Your faith trajectory starts to grow, your relationship with God starts to grow, and all of the relationships around you deepen.

Being thankful for growing relationships is not easy, but it is such an important step in knowing God. If we ignore this step of getting to know God our faith will always seem ethereal and out of touch with reality. When your faith starts to interact with every relationship in your life, you start to understand how God can and will use any relationship around you to bring you closer to Him.

REFLECTION QUESTIONS

1. Most of the time we are simply trying to keep our relationships going, instead of thinking about "growing relationships." What stood out to you from this chapter that may have confronted your idea of how relationships should look?

2. Thankfulness seems like such a weak response when there are far grander actions we could take. Yet, in this chapter we discovered thankfulness is an essential heart

transformation and very powerful antidote to selfishness. What makes it difficult to be thankful in everyday life?

3. We talked about our relationships needing to be in a certain order if we are to have growing relationships. The order is: Our relationship with God, our relationships with family, our relationship to others in the Church, and our relationships within the world. Do you find it hard to keep your relationships in this order? Why?

4. Scripture calls us to "submit to one another out of reverence for Christ." We talked about many ways submitting can be expressed in our relationships. Which one of these did you find difficult?

5. Romans 12 shows the kind of relationships we should have within the church. Have you had relationships like this within a church?

6. We talked about our own "limit of love" but how God has an endless amount of love that can fill our lives if we are willing to be thankful in the midst of testing relationships. Have you seen this "limit of love" in your own life?

7. Which of the application questions below will be most difficult for you? Why?

APPLICATION

1. Be thankful for the people God has placed in your life – Make a list of the people you interact with on a daily basis. Go through your list and write out one way you can be thankful for these people.

2. Be thankful for relationships and situations that test your own "limit of love" – Instead of running away when you face a limit of love situation this coming week, ask the Lord to give you His love for the person.

3. Be thankful every day for another opportunity to show God's love – This week, even when you do not feel like it, take some time to ask God to give you a thankful spirit and then choose to be thankful.

ENGAGE

Step 6
WAITING FOR EVERYONE TO BE EQUIPPED

Throughout this book, we have discovered how knowing God is more than just a moment. Knowing God is a process. Before we can even accept the Gospel message, God must bring us to a point of humility and brokenness. Then, when we hear the Gospel message, we must be willing to surrender to God's grace. God's grace propels us into living an authentic life through the power of the Holy Spirit and if we continue to take steps of faith we can be thankful for growing relationships. The final step in knowing God is so important, and yet it is a step some Christians do not think is essential to knowing God – waiting for everyone to be equipped.

Everyone being equipped means it is our mission as Christians to see every person on this planet know the Gospel of Jesus Christ and to be equipped to live a life of loving obedience to God. Scripture is clear that this is an essential part of knowing God, but there are some who would not live their lives with this in mind. I have met many long-time Christians who, when you ask them how many people they have shared their faith with they get confused. They do not understand why that would matter. To their understanding, they came to know Jesus at some point in their life and their goal from that point forward was to simply be as holy as possible until they went to be with Jesus for eternity. Life became a waiting game where they are just trying to survive the ups and downs of life until they get to their prize, eternity in heaven. In fact, sometimes their annoyance with this "messed-up world" makes them angry and isolated. They look holy on the outside, but when you talk to them they don't seem to express the faith, hope, and love so characteristic of Jesus. Their desire to be with Jesus for eternity is a wonderful thing, yet it is almost as if what they are waiting for is simply the prize at the end of the "game of life" instead of the final reunion with their beloved Savior. Since they are orienting their lives around their performance before God and not their relationship with God, their actions become strangely self-centered. This waiting-game attitude produces apathy in their lives in terms of sharing the Gospel with other people because it takes them away from those who do not know Jesus. If their goal is to reach heaven with as little messiness as possible, they will try to avoid any dark and broken places in the world. They would not want their minds to be influenced by people that do not know Jesus, and since they are basing everything on their own performance they would not trust themselves to stand up against temptation. Their lives become defensive and apathetic, waiting around for Jesus to come back instead of a life that changes the world for Jesus. Maybe you have met Christians like this before too. Maybe it is part of the reason that coming to faith has been so hard for you. This does not look like a life most of us would want. Maybe you are one of these Christians and you have wondered why your life feels so empty when you thought a relationship with Jesus was supposed to be fulfilling.

The New Testament clearly teaches this is not the type of life we are to be living. We are supposed to have an impact on the world as Christians. The Great Commission, what Jesus told his disciples in Matthew 28:18-20 says, "All authority in heaven and on earth has been given to me. Therefore go and make disciples of all nations, baptizing them in the name of the Father and of the Son and of the Holy Spirit, and teaching them to obey everything I have commanded you. And surely I am with you always, to the very end of the age." The mission Jesus gives to His church involves going, making, baptizing, and teaching. These are essential steps to seeing everyone become equipped. They are also essential to knowing God because if we never seek to share the Good News about Jesus, I wonder if we have really received the Good News? David Platt puts it another way: "If we're not making disciples are we really disciples?"[25] Now, I am not saying each one of us has to be an evangelist like Billy Graham, travelling around leading thousands upon thousands to Jesus. In fact, some of us may live most of our lives behind the scenes and may not even seem to make a huge impact. The question is: are we simply waiting for the end of the "game of life" or are we waiting for everyone to be equipped?

I have used the word "waiting" intentionally. There is a definitive attitude to someone who is waiting for something. When my wife and I got married, we had to have a Friday night wedding because it was the only way we could have all of our family in attendance. Many people get married on a Saturday and it is usually in the morning, which means they only have to wait for a couple hours from when they wake up until they get married. In our case, we did not get married until 6 PM which meant I had to wait all day to see Janelle. Because I was so excited and yet had to wait, I realized it did something to my attitude for the day. I was really productive, getting things done I needed to do for the wedding and the honeymoon. I cleaned the car, I packed for the honeymoon, I got paperwork in order, I made sure everything was set at the church, I got my groomsmen together – the list went on and on. Everything I did that day had one sole purpose: to be ready to marry Janelle. I was not sitting on the couch watching TV because the anticipation of what was coming would not let me sit idly by. I arrived early at all my appointments that day. I did everything to the best of my ability. I left no stone unturned in my ambition of making everything perfect for our wedding day and beyond. Since we had to get pictures with our bridal party before the wedding took place, we decided to have a moment where Janelle would walk down the aisle to me before the wedding. It was a private moment where I could finally see my bride and we could pray for what was to come. I remember being in the sanctuary early and then pacing with excitement. I had waited for so long and the expectation of marrying Janelle was finally going to be met with the reality.

This illustration demonstrates how an attitude of waiting on something is an attitude of expectation. Interestingly enough, Revelation 19 describes the end of time when Jesus comes back again to get His bride, the Church, as a marriage supper. Throughout the New Testament we are encouraged to keep our focus on this time, waiting expectantly for Jesus' return and our reception into eternal bliss with God. If we really have an attitude of expectant waiting, we will not just sit around. We will work hard to be prepared for that day. You might say, "This sounds a lot like waiting for heaven which you said brings apathy." The important distinction is the reason for our waiting. Waiting on a reward brings about expectation for the reward but apathy in our love, while waiting on God brings about an expectation of both love and reward. What we love defines how we act. If we love God, we will actively be doing anything we can to share God's love with every person we meet until our time ends on this earth.

If we are honest, however, all of us have felt this tension between apathy and expectation in our waiting. Even though we want to be actively sharing the Gospel message, it is so easy to get sidetracked. This is why our daily battle between apathy and expectation actually produces an environment for us to know God more. Remember how we said in the last chapter that in the tension of growing relationships we come to know God more? One of the most active ways for us to grow in our knowledge of God is when we are on mission with Him seeking for everyone to be equipped. In this chapter, we will look at the different ways we are called to be on mission in the world as a follower of Christ, the things that hold us back from being on mission, and suggestions of how to keep waiting for everyone to be equipped.

GO

"Go" is such a simple word and yet it can be one of the scariest words to most people. "Go" necessitates action. It demands that we break free from our comfort. "Go" means leaving behind the known to pursue the unknown. "Go" means breaking free from habits and customs and cliques. It is not easy, and yet, it is the first word of the Great Commission that Jesus gave to His disciples. Jesus viewed it as the primary step in making sure everyone was equipped. Before the death and resurrection of Jesus, the Jewish people were the only people group who served the One and Only God. They were chosen by God to be the people from whom the Messiah would come. But hundreds of years before the coming of the Messiah, Jesus, there were prophecies stating this Messiah would open up the way for God to bring salvation to all people throughout the entire world. That very thing happened after His resurrection, which is why His call is to "go and make disciples of all nations." Saving faith was now going to be available to all people through the sacrifice of Jesus.

I say all of this because it was an important reason why the word "go" was even more difficult for the disciples who Jesus talked to at the time than it might even be for us. Can you imagine how difficult it would have been for these Jewish disciples who had lived their whole lives believing they were the people of God who had to be pure and separate from the unclean Gentiles (people outside of Israel) who did not follow God? They had lived their whole lives doing all the right deeds and keeping all the right laws unlike the Gentiles. The Gentiles worshipped idols, not the one true God. Gentiles ate unclean food and often practiced despicable things. Many of the Jewish Christians may have thought it would be easier to just stick together with people like themselves and try to live the most righteous life they could (similar to the waiting-game Christians I described above). They could have even rationalized that if they did this, then the unclean Gentiles might see what they are doing and try to do the same. But Jesus didn't give them this option. He didn't want His love to be shown apathetically. He wanted as many people as possible to know about His love for them. So He called his disciples to go to "all nations." And this same call applies to us today. We may not have a struggle between Jewish and Gentile, but there are still clear divisions in our society today that if held onto will cause us to not really want *everyone* to be equipped. Even if we are not holding onto prejudices and divisions, we still may not want to go because going is uncomfortable. But according to Jesus' commands going is our only option if we really want to know God and His heart for the world.

Now you might be saying, "Okay, I get it. We are supposed to go. But go where?" We are supposed to go everywhere and anywhere God calls us to go. Everywhere you look there are dark and broken places in the world. God wants us to go to these places and provide His love. We are supposed to go to the least and the lost and provide love. We are supposed to go wherever people are disillusioned, stuck, and confused and provide truth. Ultimately, we are supposed to go to anyone who does not yet know the Gospel. This might sound overwhelming and hard to take on. You might say, "I am only one person. How could I possibly change anything in these dark places?" It is true that the task can seem daunting, but God makes a habit of doing more in and through our lives than we could have done on our own. If you are willing to offer your life up to Him and simply follow His lead when He calls you to go, amazing things will happen.

If you are still concerned about the enormity of the task God gives us, the great thing is God has already put people in our path. His first call is for us to equip, with the Gospel, those people we meet where we live, where we work, and where we play. These are places we can all identify with and a perfect place to start. Does your family know God? If not, use your time at home to live like Jesus and share the testimony of what God has done in your life. How about your neighbors? Be a good neighbor, let them know that you love them, and let them know that God loves them. What about work? Live a faithful life like Jesus at work and provide hope when everyone else seems overwhelmed. What about your gym, hobby group, or community group? Love people, live like Jesus, and let them know there are real answers to life's toughest problems. The first step in going is living with an expectant attitude that opportunities to see everyone equipped are going to happen where you live, work, or play.

The amazing thing is when you start to see the world with this mission in mind, it gives purpose and meaning to every part of your day. Most of us struggle to connect the dots between all the different aspects of our day. We feel like we are torn in twenty different directions and not sure how things really connect. God promises to connect the dots of our lives, but most of us get distracted from seeking God during any given day. Recall how many times throughout a day you really think about talking to God. Maybe you spend some time praying in the morning or in your car ride to work, but for many people God is not on the radar for most of the day. This is gravely unfortunate because if we don't practice the presence of God throughout the day, then we miss out on some of the most important ways of knowing God more. I believe the reason we do not connect God to our daily lives is because we divide our lives into sacred and secular. We believe God only meets with us when we are sitting in a room praying. Actually, you may discover as much or more about God in the midst of the work of God than you would just sitting in a room praying.

I helped to lead a trip to Haiti several years ago. It was not long after the earthquake and we were going to spend some time ministering to kids in a particular area of the country. We had a mixed group of people that came on the trip. There were people of different ages, different backgrounds, and even from different parts of the country. When we all first met we were nice to each other, but many of us were still just acquaintances. By the end of a week where we had traveled together, eaten together, slept in bunks in 100-degree weather at night, served people in many different capacities, and talked to one another about our hopes and dreams you would have thought we were family. I find this happens so often on mission trips or during events where people are working together on something because when you are working towards a common end with other people it produces a common heart. The same is true with knowing God. Everywhere God dwells is sacred and when you surrender to God's grace His Holy Spirit dwells within you. You carry God with you wherever you go and when you do not resist Him but instead join Him in His work in the world you will develop a common heart with God. When we leave God out of our "going" by refusing to seek Him on how He might want to use us in our daily lives, we are missing out on understanding His heart for the world. We are forfeiting the growth we could have as we work to show His love within the world.

Trying to change the world without His help will yield no actual transformation through our efforts. Remember, the only way transformation can happen in people is through the work of the Holy Spirit. We must take a step along with God to go into the world and reach out so that everyone can be equipped with the message of Jesus.

MAKING DISCIPLES

You might say, "Alright, so I understand what it means to

go, where I need to go, and why I need to go, but what am I supposed to do as I go?" Jesus said in the Great Commission we are to "make disciples of all nations, baptizing them in the name of the Father and of the Son and of the Holy Spirit, and teaching them to obey everything I have commanded you." We are supposed to make disciples of Jesus. Thankfully, Jesus gives us some insight into what this disciple-making process looks like.

First, we are to baptize people. Now, most of us who are reading this don't actually perform baptisms, so I am not saying you should start trying to dunk people in water. In our day and age, baptism is a symbol of a spiritual reality that has happened in our hearts. Baptism is an outward demonstration and testimony that someone has surrendered to the grace of God through the Cross. People who get baptized are declaring they have been brought from death to life and are now living a new life through the power of the Holy Spirit. All people who have committed their life to Jesus should participate in baptism, and for the most part people in our country will not face opposition for doing so. But because there are no consequences for being baptized in this day and age, many people will get baptized simply because they believe it is a good thing to do even if they are not actually living a life for God. It is very common in our world today for people to be baptized but never actually know God.

In biblical times, however, baptism was an action often accompanied by serious consequences. A person publicly confessing their faith in Jesus may have faced opposition from people because of turning away from the gods of the day. This was a serious commitment someone would not have taken lightly. So, when Matthew records Jesus talking about baptism in Matthew 28 he is not just referring to a ritual. He is explaining the commitment someone is making to engage in the same process we are talking about in this book. We are to baptize those people that can declare that they did not know God at one point in their life but they now know God. They were willing to be humbled, broken, and surrendered to God's grace. Our goal, as we go, is not just to see how many people we can get dunked in some water. Rituals never truly transform anyone. Instead, we are to help people see that Jesus is the only place they can find peace, meaning, and fulfillment. We are to share with people what Jesus did and call them to a point of decision about the grace of God. Sometimes we can share this with people quickly. Sometimes it can take years of relationship with a person to earn the right to share the Good News with them. Whatever the case, we are to be making disciples by sharing the grace of God with every person we meet.

Second, we are to make disciples by teaching people to obey everything Jesus commanded. We are not to just teach people mere knowledge and facts about Jesus, although it is good they learn them. We are to teach them to *obey* everything Jesus commanded. It is relatively easy to teach people facts. It is far harder to teach people heart lessons. I cannot tell you how many times I come across people who know the Bible inside and out, but aren't willing to obey what God has said. They could tell you the history and facts of the Bible, but they aren't willing to obey the Person the Bible is about. This was part of the reason I felt I needed to write this book, in which we have discussed engaging in the process of knowing God. The process of engaging is heart training. We have to teach people the basics of being revived, thankful, and waiting in order to teach them how to obey God. I am not claiming I have covered every heart transformation in this book that we are to teach by any means, but it is at least a start. As you have probably realized in reading this book, allowing God to transform your heart is not an easy process. It is a messy journey. When we participate in teaching others about everything Jesus has commanded us, we must participate in the journey with them.

When I think about the jobs I have held throughout my life, it is easy to distinguish between the jobs where I have truly been equipped and those where I have not. In jobs where I have not been equipped, I would simply be given a task and the boss would walk away. I would have to figure things out on my own and I would mess up a lot. I would often become disheartened because I honestly wanted to be helpful, but there was no one there to guide me. On the other hand, when I worked a job where someone walked alongside me and equipped me to do the job properly I would be so thankful for the support in the midst of learning. I might still make mistakes, but at least I had someone to walk with me through the mess. Sometimes in the church we lead people to the point of baptism and then we forget the second part of what Jesus said. We must teach people to obey everything Jesus commanded. This means walking along with people in their journey of being revived, thankful, and waiting.

Now, you might say, "That all sounds great, but there is no way that I am prepared to go out and tell people around me about these things. I barely feel equipped myself. I do not have a theology degree and can't explain things very well. What happens if they ask questions?" I could probably keep going on and on with questions and excuses because few of us feel completely qualified to share the Gospel with someone else. However, it is important for us to remember several things.

First, bringing people to salvation is not our job. Our job is simply to go and share the Good News. It is God who brings people to salvation. Imagine if I were standing outside of a ferry. The ferry was docked on one side of a lake and I knew on the other side of the lake was the most amazing place ever, where people could meet the person who created them and live a life far more amazing then they could have ever imagined. I would want to tell every person I could find to get on the ferry so they could experience what I had experienced. However, I could not force them to get on the ferry and even if they did get on the ferry there would be no way I could captain the ferry across the lake. The only action I could take is to tell people what I knew about the place and what I had experienced there. In a similar way, you cannot do anything to ultimately bring someone to salvation. You cannot force someone to love God and confess his or her need for God. Only God can work in someone to bring them to this point. Your job is simply to tell what you have experienced, what you know about salvation, and ask them to consider surrendering to God's grace.

Another important thing for you to remember if you don't feel qualified to share the Gospel is that it doesn't matter if what you share is particularly eloquent. People will not ultimately be convinced by arguments alone. All of us want to know if something works. If you have ever watched an infomercial trying to convince you to buy something, the first question we all ask is, "Does it really work?" If you are sharing the Gospel with people they will most likely be more interested if God is really doing something in your life than they are in getting an incredibly eloquent presentation of the Gospel. The Apostle Paul, in talking to the Corinthian Church in 1 Corinthians 2:1-5 said:

And so it was with me, brothers and sisters. When I came to you, I did not come with eloquence or human wisdom as I proclaimed to you the testimony about God. For I resolved to know nothing while I was with you except Jesus Christ and him crucified. I came to you in weakness with great fear and trembling. My message and my preaching were not with wise and persuasive words, but with a demonstration of the Spirit's power, so that your faith might not rest on human wisdom, but on God's power.

The Apostle Paul was one of the greatest missionaries in the history of the church. He would have known the Gospel inside and out, and yet even he seems to be a little afraid of not sharing the Gospel well. According to the second-century *Acts of Paul and Thecla,* Paul was not a particularly persuasive or charismatic character. It says he was "a man small of stature, with a baldhead and crooked legs, in a good state of body, with eyebrows meeting and nose somewhat hooked."[26] There were a lot of things going against him being persuasive in sharing the Gospel. Yet, he says in the end he was not trying to look particularly wise or persuasive so people would accept Jesus because of him. He simply wanted to be a demonstration of the Spirit's power so people could understand that it was God who was doing the work in His life. In this case with the Corinthians, the fact God had changed his life even though he was not particularly special seemed to be what let them know that God could work in their life too.

It is important to know how to explain the Gospel and how to share what happens because of it in our lives. It is part of the reason this book was written. But, in the end, the testimony of your journey and the testimony of your godly life lived out in front of people will be the most persuasive things that will draw people to Jesus. If they see how Jesus worked in your life to bring about the things they have always desired, they will be more likely to receive the gift of salvation. So in order to have everyone equipped we must all go out and make disciples. This involves being willing to call people to a point of surrender to God's grace and then teach them how to live out their faith. This is done best by loving people, sharing our testimony with them, and offering to walk beside them in their journey toward faith.

HOW DO I WAIT FOR EVERYONE TO BE EQUIPPED?

Hopefully, at this point, you understand why we need to be on mission to see everyone equipped. Hopefully you understand where we need to go and what we need to do as we go. Hopefully, you even understand why waiting for everyone to be equipped is an essential heart attitude in our lives and how we actually come to know God better as we live this way. However, you may still be wondering how we are to live out this waiting lifestyle? There are at least three ways I believe we can develop a waiting heart.

1. Wait on the Lord.

The heart attitude of waiting to see everyone be equipped is really a barometer of our own relationship with God. If we understand what God has done for us through Jesus, if we understand what God currently wants to do for us, and if we understand what will happen to those who do not know God, then the expectation we have to see everyone be equipped with faith should be one of the greatest desires of our heart every day. It must be at the center of everything we do, everything we are, and everything we dream about. If it is not the greatest passion of our hearts, then we can either assume we do not really know and understand what Jesus offers to all people, or we can assume we have become impatient and distracted by other idols.

The desire and the power to reach others for God begins with a thriving relationship with God. We have already talked in this book about many ways we can establish a thriving relationship with God. In Psalm 40:1-3 we see another way of establishing a thriving relationship with Jesus:

> *I waited patiently for the Lord;*
> *He turned to me and heard my cry.*
> *He lifted me out of the slimy pit,*
> *out of the mud and mire;*
> *He set my feet on a rock*
> *and gave me a firm place to stand.*
> *He put a new song in my mouth,*
> *a hymn of praise to our God.*
> *Many will see and fear the Lord*
> *and put their trust in Him.*

This is a psalm King David wrote when he was in a bad place. He feels stuck and I would imagine he did not feel very excited about reaching out to others. He says that he is stuck in the mud and the mire. Maybe you feel like you are stuck in the mud and the mire like David expressed. Even if you wanted to reach out to others to help them know God, you do not feel qualified because your life feels like a mess. When King David was in this position, he stopped to wait patiently for the Lord.

Sometimes the affections of our heart get in the wrong order. Sometimes we become impatient and run back to idols in our life because they are easier to deal with and provide us with temporary comfort. In these times, we must stop everything and simply wait on the Lord, like David did. If waiting is synonymous with expecting, then waiting on the Lord would be putting ourselves before God expecting Him to do something in us that we cannot do ourselves. We cannot pull ourselves out of the slimy pit we are stuck in. We need God. Part of the reason I have periodically lost the desire to see everyone equipped in my life is because I lose sight of the very basics of what God has done in me. When I choose to bring myself before the Lord and wait to hear from Him about what is going on in my life I often find that I have lost sight of being humbled, broken, surrendered, revived, or thankful. One or all of these heart attitudes has gotten out of order in my life. God faithfully points this out to me as I wait on Him and as I release to Him what I have been holding onto I find freedom from the slimy pit of selfishness and the mud and mire of the idols I had turned my attention toward.

What is exciting about this is that when I choose to confess this to God and remember that all good things flow from Him, my excitement and desire to tell other people about His goodness returns. In Psalm 40, as David is released from the mud and the mire, he says God puts a "new song" in his heart that ends up pointing other people back to God. One of my housemates in college loved to sing. He was a great friend and one of the things I loved about him is if you started singing the first couple notes of a song he would finish it out (no matter what song it was). One semester at school, I decided to make a game of it. I talked to my other housemates and we set a particular amount of time for this challenge. The goal would be to see how many times one of us could get our friend to start singing with us. We kept an informal tally in one of our rooms. Some days we would be sitting in a common room and you would watch as each one of us took turns starting the lyrics of a song seeing if we could get our friend to start singing. More often than not he would join in. Now, before you think I am a terrible guy for doing this to my friend, we ended up telling him about the challenge and he thought it was funny. But he taught me something through it as well. He was so willing to start singing because he had a song in his heart already. His love for God was evident in how he conducted his life and how he loved people. He brought a certain joy to those around him because of the joy he had from God.

Our lives are similarly contagious if God puts a "new song" in our hearts. If you do not feel like waiting for everyone to be equipped, then wait on the Lord until He puts a "new song" in your heart.

2. Wait in prayer for others.

Let's be honest and admit something we have not really acknowledged this entire chapter: The vast majority of us are not good at waiting. In fact, some of us would rather do anything at all other than wait. Let us fix the situation. Let us go out there and fight a battle. Let us go hide. Just do not ask us to intentionally wait on something. For some of us, this is actually what is keeping us from seeing everyone in our lives equipped with the Gospel. We might falter at waiting on God, but we also might falter in waiting in prayer for others. What I mean is that some of us might hear that we are to be out there sharing God's love and message with the world and we take it to heart. We start serving at every church event we can, we start handing out tracts to people, we initiate (sometimes awkward) conversations with people about Jesus, and we try to find open doors of sharing the Gospel everywhere we go. Most of this is not bad. In fact, we should be doing some of these things. The problem is, if we never wait in prayer for others how do we know we are reaching out to them in the right way? If we never ask God what He wants us to do for others, how do we know we are expending our energies in the right direction? If we never pray for a sensitivity to understand someone else and their situation, how do we know we will not turn them away from the Gospel more than bring them close to the Gospel? Most importantly, it is only by the power of God that someone is truly brought to salvation. The Bible says in 1 Peter 5:8, "...Our enemy the devil prowls around like a roaring lion looking for someone to devour." He is going to fight against efforts for every person to come to a saving knowledge of Jesus Christ. There is a spiritual battle going on behind the scenes, which is the real battle that needs to be won. We cannot, by unspiritual methods, bring about spiritual results. Prayer and the Word of God are the weapons we must use to fight for peoples' souls.

One of the easiest methods I have found to keep waiting in prayer for people is to keep a running list of people somewhere that you will regularly see. On this list, put people at different steps of their spiritual journey. Maybe you have a friend who is an ardent atheist and hates God. Maybe there is someone in your family that is a skeptic and does not really know what to think about God. Maybe there are others around you on a daily basis that are closer to understanding how to know God. Maybe there are still others around you who claim to know God, but do not live life in a way reflective of that. Keep them on that list and wait in prayer for them. Pray that God would open their eyes to see Him as He is. Pray with expectation believing God can use the circumstances of their life to testify to His grace for them. Pray that God would use you in whatever way He would see fit to minister to them. Listen to what He would ask of you and follow His leading. Post this list around your house at different places or in your car or on your desk. When we choose not to wait on God about others, we either rush ahead of God's plans or lag behind God's plans for other people. By choosing to put these people down on a piece of paper, we are committing ourselves to be reminded about our mission to see everyone equipped and reminded how they can only be saved through the work of God.

3.   Wait with Other Believers.

Ecclesiastes 4:9-10 says, "Two are better than one, because they have a good return for their labor: If either of them falls down, one can help the other up. But pity anyone who falls and has no one to help them up." I have found this to be true as well in waiting for everyone to be equipped. When I am waiting on God in expectation with other people I am encouraged to keep going even when I do not feel like it. I have someone by my side to remind me of the mission when I get sidetracked. I have someone to partner with in reaching out to others. I cannot thank God enough for the godly friends and mentors throughout my life who have helped me keep my heart and life in the right direction. And most of the success I have had in seeing people in my life equipped with the Gospel has come as a result of continued times of discussion, prayer, and ministry with other believers who are interested in the same thing.

Do not be deceived, however, that waiting with other

believers happens by accident. This kind of relationship has to be intentionally sought after and tempered by the fire of God's passion and difficult challenges that are shared. Imagine there were two friends that grew up together. They played together, attended school together, and would consider each other to be their best friend. Most of their conversations centered around the situations of the day, picking on each other, and their likes and dislikes. Now imagine that they are both drafted and sent off to war. Do you think their conversations and focus would be different while they were at war? They may have thought they would do anything for each other before, but now their lives are actually on the line. The stakes could not be higher. They may have believed they were best friends before, but they would soon find out what they had before is only a shadow of what could be. The perceived environment of a relationship changes the focus of that relationship.

In a similar way, if you are a believer you might think you have a lot of close friends who are like-minded and would encourage you to wait for everyone to be equipped. Unfortunately, if we do not understand the environment we are actually living in we will miss out on this kind of relationship. Most of us do not see that there is a spiritual battle going on around us at this very moment. Every second, around each one of us, people are losing their battle with cancer, others are considering suicide because their lives seems worthless, others are being destroyed by addiction, others are living hypocritical and broken lives, others are taking out their pain and rage on their children, and others are simply lost and do not know where to go. When we as believers take our eyes off this great spiritual battle surrounding us and instead keep our attention on worldly measures of success or simply staying comfortable in our bubble, our relationships will stay static.

We will not push each other to keep growing. We will not see the desperate need to have relationships with other people where we willingly confess our sins to one another, where there is an openness to lovingly challenge each other, and where we consistently pray for one another.

If you do understand the environment and want to establish a relationship with someone else like this, then it takes waiting with them. Intentionally set aside time on a regular basis where you go deeper than the normal conversations that dominate our lives with other people. Have some questions you ask one another every time you get together. John Wesley set up groups that would gather for this very purpose: to ask questions of each other's spiritual lives. Maybe use the questions he used for these times. Maybe use a couple Scriptures that are important to each one of you and ask questions based on those. If nothing else, consider using the heart transformation steps from this book as the focus of your time together:

- **Humbled by God's Eternal Truth** – Have you been struggling with submitting to God in humility?
- **Broken to Have a New Heart** – In what ways have you sinned since we last met? Are you seeking God's grace in these areas?
- **Surrendered to God's Grace** – Are you struggling with surrendering to God's grace in any way? Are you remembering that God loves you and that you can trust Him?
- **Revived for Authentic Living** – Are there any places where you are saying "no" to God right now?
- **Thankful for Growing Relationships** – Are your relationships in order right now? Are you continuing

to be thankful for the relationships God has placed in your life?

- **Waiting for Everyone to Be Equipped** – Are you connecting your everyday life with the mission of God? Are you expecting God to work in your life to bring other people to Himself?

You might say, "This seems really intense!" But again, if we understand the situation this world is in and how desperately God wants others to see His love, then these relationships with people who are waiting with us can become some of the most cherished relationships we will ever have. If you start to pursue this intentionally with some other people in your life, you will find over time that you start to do it naturally and on a regular basis. Waiting with other believers can become a lifestyle.

Whether it is waiting on God, waiting in prayer for others, or waiting with other believers (or all of the above), I encourage you to be waiting for everyone to be equipped. As we do, let us "trust as if the whole thing depended on God and work as if the whole thing depended on us."[27]

REFLECTION QUESTIONS

1. This chapter says making disciples is an essential part of knowing God. Do you believe this is true?

2. Waiting was connected with expectation in this chapter. What stops you from living your life with expectation of what God is going to do in the world around you?

3. One of the ideas behind this heart change is when you are on a mission with someone, you get to know them faster then you would otherwise. Have you seen this in your life

before? Why do you think we can see this truth in other relationships we have, but not as easily in our relationship with God?

4. Do you get nervous when you hear the word, "Go?" Why do you think those feelings arise?

5. We have to remember that we are not called to save people. We are simply called to share the Good News and let God save people. Does this take some of the pressure off when you think about making disciples?

6. The heart attitude of waiting is really a barometer of our own faith. If we do not see a desire in our hearts for others know God, then we must be struggling with one of the other steps of knowing God. Have you seen this in your own life before?

7. Which of the application questions below will be most difficult for you? Why?

APPLICATION

1. Wait on the Lord – If you are not passionate about waiting for everyone to be equipped wait on the Lord in prayer. Read Psalm 40 and cry out to God like David did.

2. Wait in prayer for others – Follow the instructions in the chapter and start a list of people to pray for on a regular basis.

3. Wait with other believers – Start to form relationships with other believers like this chapter suggests. Look for another person who could be an accountability partner for you and start meeting together. Ask loving but tough questions of each other and pray for one another.

Conclusion
HOW TO SHARE THE GOSPEL

This book started with a premise that knowing God does not just happen in a moment. Knowing God is a process. There are some who think that just because they recited a prayer at one point in their life or because they participated in some sort of ritual that they know God and are going to be with Him in eternity. Yet, many of these same people have lives that look nothing like God and they are not experiencing the love, meaning, and purpose that is supposed to accompany a relationship with God. We have discovered in this book that there are prescribed heart transformations that happen inside each person that comes to know God. For many of these people, they may be deceived that they know God because they have never understood what the Gospel really meant for their life. There are many ways to share the Gospel and I believe the church universal does a good job of describing what Jesus did for us. Unfortunately, I do not think we always do a good job of describing how we need to respond to Who God is and what He has done.

Despite this, many people have still accepted the Gospel

and have learned either by experience or further teaching what happened in their heart to bring them into a relationship with God. There are many others, however, that I think dismiss the message of the Gospel because we are not clear about what has to take place inside of us in order to know God. My conviction in writing this book is if we could clearly and easily communicate this message to those around us, many more would come to a saving knowledge of God. In order to aid in that process, I came up with a series of symbols that are easy to write and could uniquely communicate the Gospel through the heart changes that must take place in us. You may have noticed them at the beginning of each chapter throughout the book. I pray they could be used to at least give you a framework of understanding so that as you talk to other people you might be able to express the Gospel clearly. Also, I have imagined it would be an easy way to write out the Gospel for someone on a napkin at a meal or on a piece of paper as you're having a discussion. I will write each symbol below and give an explanation of why I think each one communicates the heart change it represents.

HUMBLED BY GOD'S ETERNAL TRUTH

If we are to ever know God, the first step that must happen in our lives is to be willing to humble ourselves enough to accept that there is a God. To be humbled is to be brought down from our place of pride and brought to a place of being willing to accept that we do not know everything (symbolized by the arrow pointing downward). We must we willing to humble ourselves to admit that there are absolute truths beyond simply what we think or feel, to admit there is an eternity beyond this world, and to admit there might be a God Who has answers we've been seeking.

"Humble yourselves, therefore, under God's mighty hand, that he may lift you up in due time." – 1 Peter 5:6

BROKEN TO HAVE A NEW HEART

After we are willing to be humbled, we must come to terms with our own lives. Are we really as good as we think we are? The Bible says we are sinful people who need a new heart. If we are willing to really consider our lives, we will find that through all the twists and turns there are sinful patterns and empty places in our souls. We are not the "good" people we thought we were, and instead are in desperate need of someone to save us from ourselves. If we are willing to acknowledge the fact that we are sinful and need a new heart before God then we are moving ever closer to knowing God and finding salvation (symbolized by the jagged and broken arrow pointing downward).

"...For all have sinned and fall short of the glory of God" – Romans 3:23

SURRENDER TO GOD'S GRACE

After we are humbled and broken we come to a crossroad (which is one of the things the Y represents). The decision we have to make at that crossroad is whether we will surrender our lives to God or continue to pursue our own path. God wants to pour His grace into our lives to give us a new heart and welcome us into a relationship with Him (which the Y also represents by having an opening at the top). This grace is possible because Jesus, God's Son, was willing to receive the punishment that we deserved for our sin even though He had lived a perfect life. He died for us on the Cross, and then against all odds rose again from the dead. Because He conquered sin and death, we can now find forgiveness for our sins and life with God for eternity if we are willing to say "Yes" (another thing the Y represents) to God and surrender our lives to Him.

"For it is by grace you have been saved, through faith—and this is not from yourselves, it is the gift of God— not by works, so that no one can boast." – Ephesians 2:8-9

REVIVED FOR AUTHENTIC LIVING

Surrendering to God's grace is not the end of the Gospel and not the end of the story when it comes to knowing God. When we enter into a relationship with God, He gives us His Holy Spirit to point our lives toward Heaven (one thing the symbol represents). Also, if we let Him, He takes the many conflicting parts of our lives and brings them into a single focus (represented by how the symbol goes from two lines to one). As we are revived, our lives begin to look more and more like Jesus every day. We begin to learn what it is like to walk with God (if you draw in hands and a head, the symbol looks like a person walking).

"So then, just as you received Christ Jesus as Lord, continue to live your lives in him, rooted and built up in him, strengthened in the faith as you were taught, and overflowing with thankfulness." – Colossians 2:6-7

THANKFUL FOR GROWING RELATIONSHIPS

As God starts to revive us, our relationships start to change. Relationships are not static and there are twists and turns in them (represented in the jagged lines of the symbol). Many of our relationships are broken and not growing in the way God desires. If we start to invest in our relationships in the correct order of God, family, church, and others, our relationships start to grow in the way God intended. When we cultivate an attitude of thankfulness in the tension of growing relationships, God will start to fill in the gaps of our relationships (represented by drawing a line through the broken line of the symbol). We will end up knowing God more by continuing to be thankful as we grow in our relationships, and God will use those relationships to point our hearts and minds toward Heaven (symbolized by the arrow at the top of the symbol).

"Rejoice always, pray continually, give thanks in all circumstances; for this is God's will for you in Christ Jesus." – 1 Thessalonians 5:16-18

WAITING FOR EVERYONE EQUIPPED

The end result of this work of God in our lives is that we desire to share the Gospel with other people. We live in expectation of Jesus' return to the earth and because of this expectation we live our life pointed toward heaven to show others the way (symbolized by the arrow pointing up). We wait on God, seeking His strength as we go and make disciples of all nations.

"All authority in heaven and on earth has been given to me. Therefore go and make disciples of all nations, baptizing them in the name of the Father and of the Son and of the Holy Spirit, and teaching them to obey everything I have commanded you. And surely I am with you always, to the very end of the age." – Matthew 28:18-20

This book began with a story about a waiting room and a moth: a representation that most of us are lost and searching for true meaning, peace, and love. I pray you have become convinced that you will never find true meaning, peace, and love unless you engage in knowing God. I pray you have become encouraged to take steps of faith. If you were not a believer when you started this book, I pray you have chosen to surrender to God's grace. If you are already a Christian I pray you were encouraged that sharing the wonderful news of Jesus is not as hard as you thought. I will be asking God to guide you as you continue your journey. Let me leave you with the words of the famous missionary Jim Elliot: "He is no fool who gives what he cannot keep to gain that which he cannot lose."[28]

[1] "Universe Statistics," Statistic Brain, accessed February 2, 2017, http://www.statisticbrain.com/universe-statistics/.

[2] Sebastian Anthony, "Astronomers estimate 100 Billion habitable Earth-like planets in the Milky Way, 50 Sextillion in the Universe," Extreme Tech, April 4, 2013, accessed on February 2, 2017, https://www.extremetech.com/extreme/152573-astronomers-estimate-100-billion-habitable-earth-like-planets-in-the-milky-way-50-sextillion-in-the-universe.

[3] Deborah Byrd, "How long to travel to Alpha Centauri?" SPACE, April 29, 2016, accessed on February 2, 2017, http://earthsky.org/space/alpha-centauri-travel-time.

[4] Clara Moskowitz, "What's 96 Percent of the Universe Made of? Astronomers Don't Know," SPACE.com, May 12, 2011, accessed on February 2, 2017, http://www.space.com/11642-dark-matter-dark-energy-4-percent-universe-panek.html.

[5] C.S. Lewis, *Mere Christianity* (1952; San Francisco: HarperSanFrancisco, 2001).

[6] G.K. Chesterton, *What's Wrong with the World*, (1910; Ignatius Press, October 1, 1994).

[7] St. Augustine, *The Confessions*, (Peabody: Hendrickson Publishers Inc., 2004), Book 1.

[8] "Transplants By Organ Type January 1, 1988 - December 31, 2016," United Network for Organ Sharing, accessed February 1, 2017, https://www.unos.org/data/.

[9] Gerald Cowen, "Heart," *Holman Illustrated Bible Dictionary* (Nashville, Tennessee: Holman Bible Publishers, 2003)

[10] Simon Shuster, "The World's Deadliest Drug: Inside a Krokodil Cookhouse," Time Magazine, December 5, 2013, accessed February 1, 2017, http://time.com/3398086/the-worlds-deadliest-drug-inside-a-krokodil-cookhouse/.

[11] "What's a Student Loan Grace Period?," Goodbye Loans, accessed February 1, 2017,

https://www.goodbyeloans.com/loan-forgiveness/student-loan-grace-period/.

[12] Francis Foulkes, "Ephesians: An Introduction and Commentary," in *Tyndale Commentary*, ed. Leon Morris (Illinois: Intervarsity Press, 1989), 80-81.

[13] "The Nicene Creed," United States Conference of Catholic Bishops, accessed February 1, 2017, http://www.usccb.org/beliefs-and-teachings/what-we-believe/.

[14] Danny Groner, "Ten Athletes Who Guaranteed Victory…and How Their Predictions Fared," TSM Interactive, July 26, 2012, accessed February 1, 2017, http://tsminteractive.com/10-athletes-who-guaranteed-victory/.

[15] "Namath 'Guarantees' for Jets but Coach Ewbank Not as Confident," The Press-Courier, January 11, 1969, accessed February 1, 2017, https://news.google.com/newspapers?id=oxxSAAAAIBAJ&sjid=eDQNAAAAIBAJ&pg=6628,2259168&dq=guarantees+victory&hl=en.

[16] Lewis, *Mere Christianity*, 55-56.

[17] "A 'Twelve Facts' Resurrection Logic Puzzle," ThinkApologetics.com, July 8, 2011, accessed February 2, 2017, https://chab123.wordpress.com/2011/07/08/a-twelve-facts-resurrection-logic-puzzle/.

[18] E. Stanley Jones, quoted in *Sacred Symbols that Speak*, Anthony Coniaris (Light and Life publishing company, 1987)

[19] Paul Jackson, "Holy Spirit," *Holman Illustrated Bible Dictionary* (Nashville, Tennessee: Holman Bible Publishers, 2003)

[20] Richard Foster, *Celebration of Discipline* (New York: HarperCollins Publishers, 1988), 7.

[21] Dallas Willard, *The Spirit of the Disciplines: Understanding How God Changes Lives*, (HarperOne, May 5, 1999), 353.

[22] Derek Kidner, "Genesis: An Introduction and

Commentary," in *Tyndale Commentary*, ed. Donald Wiseman (Illinois: Intervarsity Press, 1967), 70.

[23] Psalm 127:3 from *The New Living Translation*

[24] Leslie Haggin Geary, "Retirement Planning for 20-Somethings," Bankrate, accessed February 2, 2017, http://www.bankrate.com/finance/financial-literacy/retirement-planning-for-20-somethings-1.aspx.

[25] David Platt quoted by Jordan White, "Real Disciples Make Disciples," Revolution Church, April 8, 2015, accessed February 2, 2017, http://revolution.church/sermon/real-disciples-make-disciples/.

[26] Leon Morris, "1 Corinthians: An Introduction and Commentary," in *Tyndale Commentary*, ed. Leon Morris (Illinois: Intervarsity Press, 1985), 56.

[27] E. Stanley Jones, "The Habit of Reading the Bible Daily," in *Devotional Classics*, ed. Richard J. Foster and James Bryan Smith (New York: HarperCollins Publishers, 1990), 281-282.

[28] Jim Elliot quoted by Justin Taylor, "He was No Fool," The Gospel Coalition, January 8, 2010, accessed February 2, 2017, https://blogs.thegospelcoalition.org/justintaylor/2010/01/08/he-ws-no-fool/

Made in the USA
Middletown, DE
27 February 2017